GREENWORKS

GREENWORKS
Tender Loving Care for Plants

JUDITH HANDELSMAN
SARA BAERWALD

ILLUSTRATIONS BY
EDUARDO ROMAN MORAS

COLLIER BOOKS
A Division of Macmillan Publishing Co., Inc
New York
COLLIER MACMILLAN PUBLISHERS
London

Macmillan Publishing Co., Inc.
866 Third Avenue, New York, N.Y. 10022
Collier-Macmillan Canada Ltd.

Greenworks is also published in a hardcover
edition by Macmillan Publishing Co., Inc.

Library of Congress
Catalog Card Number: 73–1854

First Collier Books Edition 1974
Fourth Printing 1974

Printed in the United States of America

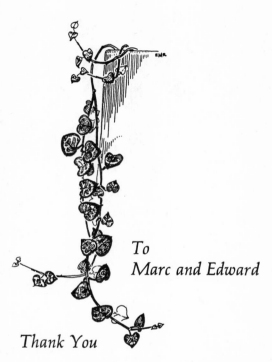

To
Marc and Edward

Thank You

Sheila at A New Leaf, The New York Horticultural Society, Pot'n' Plant, Ann, Nina, Moe, Herman, Shirley, Sam, Matt, Mossa, Cousin Dick, Dan, Teri, Arthur, Paul, Betty, Lucy, Marty, Susan, Dorothea, Lee, Sheila, Charles, Barbara, Harold, Max, Vicki, Lois, David, Peter, Larry, Gail, Carlene, Fran, Robert S., Susie, Georg-Ann, Eric, Jill, Bob, Betsy, and Tommy, Ilene, Connie, Eduardo.

CONTENTS

1. DON'T BE AFRAID OF YOUR
   PLANTS   1

2. LIGHT: ALL THERE IS TO KNOW   3
   Natural Light   4
   Exposures   6
   Artificial Light   8

3. DAILY CARE AND ROUTINES   12
   Watering   12
   Spraying   15
   Cleaning   16

4. TWENTY NO-HASSLE PLANTS   19
   Dracaena   20
   Philodendron   23
   Cast-Iron Plant   26
   False Aralia   27
   Succulents   28
   Cacti   32
   Columnea   35
   Prayer Plant   36
   Umbrella Tree   39
   Velvet Plant   41
   Spathiphyllum   42
   Sansevieria   44

    Peperomia   47
    Spider Plant   49
    Marble Queen   51
    Dumb Cane   53
    Aluminum Plant   55
    Monstera   57
    Nepthytis   59
    Palms   60

5. KEEPING YOUR PLANTS GOING ONCE THEY'VE GOTTEN STARTED   65
    Pinching   65
    Cutting Back   67
    Repotting   72
    Pots   79
    Soil   83
    Feeding   85
    Pests   90

6. NINETEEN OTHER PLANTS   97
    Asparagus Fern   97
    Ferns   99
    Staghorn Fern   103
    Jade Plant   104
    Rosary Vine   107
    Ivy   108
    African Violets   111
    Zebra Plant   113
    Piggyback Plant   115
    Coleus   118
    Geranium   120
    Ficus   122
    Swedish Ivy   125

Croton   128
Begonia   130
Fittonia   134
Wandering Jew   135
Caladium   138
Norfolk Island Pine   139

7. PROPAGATION: MAKING MORE FROM
   WHAT YOU'VE GOT   142
       Stem Cutting   142
       Leaf Cutting   146
       Division   146
       Air-Layering   148
       Winding and Pinning   151

8. STARTING FROM SCRATCH   154
       An Avocado:
           Don't Throw Away the Pit   154
       A Yam: Instead of Eating It ...   161
       A Terrarium: How to ...   167
       A New Plant: What to Look For   170

9. WHAT TO DO WHEN YOU GO
   AWAY   172
       Weekends and Vacations   172
       After-the-Weekend Blues   175

NINE OVERSIMPLIFICATIONS   177

FOURTEEN PRETTY POISONOUS
   PLANTS   179

INDEX   180

This book is for people who don't realize they have the intuition, the proverbial "green thumb," to grow flourishing plants. Before you know it, you will have learned as much as the next person about the care and maintenance of houseplants. You will be able to apply what you know about a specific plant toward general care, and vice versa. All it takes is a little interest, lots of looking, gentle touching, and the confidence to know that it will come to you in time. Plants need basically the same thing as you do. Air, water, food, light, and love. This doesn't mean you have to have extensive out-loud conversations with your plants for them to grow. Chatting isn't going to take the place of basic care vital for life. People have advised talking to plants as a way of insuring healthy growth. If you are caring for their physical needs with gentleness and concern, then you are talking to them. Plants pick up vibrations from people and their environment. They are sensitive living things. If there is chaos and tension around them, they are probably not getting the attention they need. Their looks will reflect the state of affairs. As long as they are treated as if they are alive, they *will* flourish.

People think their plants will remain the same as the day they were purchased. After all, the plant man said so, as long as they're watered "every three days." Plants need more than a splash every few days. They need cleaning, pruning, thoughtful watering, and a general attentiveness on your part. At first this may sound like a burden, but after the initial period of adjustment, you will *want* to do these things for your plants because they will show such incredible appreciation.

Green works. Green will work for you.

2 LIGHT: ALL THERE IS TO KNOW

Plant books and plant people always seem to launch into lengthy explanations of light and what kind of light is necessary for what kind of plant. They overwhelm you with the direction of your windows, hours of sunlight, and number of footcandles. I never understood what all these things meant when it came down to applying them to me and my plants. I ended up becoming totally intimidated by the complexity of the discussion and the unfamiliarity of the terms. This does not have to happen to you. Anyone can grow plants in whatever light conditions exist. The most important thing is to want to. You have to be prepared to take care of the plants both physically and emotionally. You can have the best lighting and growing conditions possible, but if you don't take care of your plants, you can bet they won't survive more than a few weeks. Growing plants in your home need not be the mysterious experience it is made out to be. Once you stop thinking there's a secret that everyone else knows but isn't telling, the better off you and your plants will be. Assessing the whole topic of light is a good place to start.

Once you have cleared up the confusion that surrounds proper lighting, you can adjust your situation accordingly. If your natural light is poor, you can still resort to artificial light or simply accept the fact that there are only a limited number of plants that will tolerate this condition. Either way, you can still have plants if you want to.

NATURAL LIGHT

For the purpose of this book the quality of natural light is divided into three categories; *direct light; filtered, or indirect, light; and darkness or shade.* This is a very simplistic breakdown of what most people consider an extremely complicated subject, but it is really all you need to know to get along, at least at first. These are broad categories into which anyone's home lighting can fit. A description of each follows, with technicalities kept to a minimum, so don't be tempted to skip this chapter, as I usually do.

Darkness or Shade. Anyone who lives in a city apartment on the main floor, in a basement flat, or on an air shaft doesn't need to be told what this category is all about. This means you can't tell what the weather is even when you go to the window and strain your neck. I lived in a ground-floor apartment with a gate on the outside of the only window in the place for two years, yet I still grew plants. The gate blocked what little light was not cut off by the buildings across the street and the trees on the sidewalk. It was a dark apartment even at the window. I contented myself with plants that grew without much light: nepthytis, philodendron, a dracaena or two, and a sansevieria. Nothing looked terribly impressive, but they all lived. Their size didn't increase much because of the lack

4

of light, but they were living things in what otherwise might have been a dreary apartment.

Any area far away from a sunny window falls into this category There's nothing like a foliage plant or tree in a shady corner of a room to add color and life. There are plants that will remain healthy and even thrive in a relatively dim corner. Dracaenas are perfect examples of foliage plants that are lush and abundant in character yet do not require much light. They are hearty and will flourish in the corners of a room, relying only on infrequent doses of light from the window or of artificial light from whatever happens to be used normally.

Filtered, Bright, or Indirect Light. The terms "filtered," "bright," and "indirect" here mean essentially the same thing. Such lighting can occur in front of any window, depending on obstructions. Bright light is not direct sunlight but light that is filtered and dispersed. Your windows may have direct sunlight at certain hours of the day but at others only the bright light described here. Many plants can flourish in this environment. Except for flowering plants, which require a great deal of sun, most foliage plants will be healthy and happy without direct sunlight. If you are lucky enough to have a southern exposure, which provides direct sunlight most of the day, areas of the room far away from the window will have bright light rather than shade. As long as the leaves of the plants are not in shade but are basking in some light, you've got enough light to grow a very large variety of plants.

Direct Light or Sunlight. This means just what it says: direct rays of the sun falling on all or many leaves of the plant. This may occur only for a few hours a day, depending on your exposure, but nevertheless there is sunlight cast directly on the plant, a must for flowering plants.

EXPOSURES

There is no reason why you should abide by any absolute rules about which way your window faces. Different kinds of light come through your windows, depending upon the way they face. The direction in which your window faces gives its name to that exposure. For example, a "northern exposure" means your window faces north. This may sound obvious at first, but there are many variables to take into account along with the direction of your window. Just because your window has a northern exposure doesn't mean you receive the maximum amount of light that the exposure affords. You may have large trees, other houses, tall buildings, or drapes and blinds blocking a certain amount of light from entering your room, so don't immediately assume if your window faces a certain direction, you will get all the light that is coming to you. Once you have read the description of the four possible exposures, it is up to you to figure out approximately how much light your plants will get. Take into consideration all the additional conditions and judge with your eyes what your light situation is. After all is said and done, you will be able to narrow your conditions down to one of the three categories mentioned.

Some of the plant literature mentions measuring your natural-light intensity in footcandles. This requires a special footcandle meter or photographic light meter and a conversion table. This is really unnecessary when trying to determine how much light you get. It is much simpler, and just as effective, to use the information at hand and some common sense in assessing your situation. Here is an uncomplicated summary of the four exposures for you to use as a guideline.

Northern Exposure. If your window faces north, you will *never* have direct sun. However, there will be good bright light all day long if the window is not obstructed by trees, buildings, houses, gates, or blinds. You can grow almost anything in this light except plants that specifically require some sunlight, like jade plants, cacti, geraniums, crotons, succulents, and English ivy. There are also many plants that will do fine in this light with the aid of an artificial lamp.

Eastern Exposure. In an unobstructed east window, plants will receive direct sunlight for a few hours in the morning and fairly low light the rest of the day. Morning sunlight is strong, but not as hot as afternoon sunlight. This is the minimum amount for a plant that needs lots of direct light.

Western Exposure. Western exposure provides good, bright light all day long and strong sunlight in the afternoon. This is an advantage over eastern light because the light is brighter for more of the time. The sun also gives off greater heat in the afternoon. As long as the sky is not obstructed by trees or other houses, the sun will come shining through.

Southern Exposure. Southern exposure is considered to be the most desirable because it provides direct sunlight almost all day. If you have only southern exposure, a variety of plants can be kept far away from the window and still get enough light. You must decide whether a corner, out of the direct rays of the sun, is brightly lit or in shade. If you like flowering plants and don't want to use artificial lights, southern exposure is just about the only thing to have. However, don't place fragile plants right in the window. Plants such as ferns and African violets will fade, burn, and wilt in direct sun. (This does not include asparagus fern, which flourishes in direct sunlight.) A good deal of heat is generated by direct sunlight, so be sure those plants sitting in a south window won't bleach or fade in color. This subject is dealt with in chapters 4 and 6.

ARTIFICIAL LIGHT

After you have assessed your lighting conditions, you can either stick with plants that match what you have or turn to artificial lighting. Some plants do well under minimal lighting conditions but would certainly appreciate a boost from an artifical source. When I first started buying plants, I felt a great pressure to go out and buy fancy artificial-lighting equipment. Plant books and pamphlets from plant shops made it sound like all my plants would die if I didn't run out immediately to buy $50 worth of reflector or fluorescent fixtures. This is unfair to a gardener just starting out and is a ridiculous assumption anyway. If your home does not have sufficient light, there are several simple and inexpensive solutions that will make you and your plants very happy. (Remember, it's the bulb that gives off the light; unless you are interested in special decorating accessories, the fixture is not what is important when choosing an artificial light.)

Fluorescent Tubes. Cool white fluorescent tubes are considered the most beneficial artificial light there is for plants. Of all the light possibilities, the fluorescent tube gives off the least amount of heat. Most lights generate a tremendous amount of heat if left on for a long period of time. Fluorescents are usually not portable, so that once they are set up, it is difficult to move them around. If you don't want to spend much money, this may not be the thing for you. Fluorescents look best in some special fixture because they produce a strong glare. They are handiest when arranged inside a glass box, like a terrarium with lights, to house very temperamental plants, such as African violets. So, while fluorescents are the finest product, they are not the most flexible item you can purchase.

Reflector Floods. These bulbs come in different wattages and cost from $1 to $4. A 150-watt flood is big enough. It can be put into any of the simple fixtures in a wide range of shapes and sizes that can be bought at any hardware store for a few dollars. The metal bowl-type fixture can clip on to just about anything and, with the help of an extension cord, can go anywhere in your house. It is not a good idea to put this light close to the foilage, since the heat from the bulb may burn or dry the leaves. If you want to leave the light on all day, place the fixture four to five feet from the plants. This will provide plenty of light and not too much heat.

If any of your lamps already have reflector floods, move them into the plant area and leave them on for several hours a day. If your lamps have reflector "spots," it will be best to change them. Reflector spots very quickly heat the area they are directed toward.

I once left a wall fixture with a reflector spot facing a bouquet of flowers and greens for the day. When I got home all the leaves had burned into a brown and yellow mess. The flowers had long since shriveled and died. Reflector floods will offer a safer, more dispersed light.

Duro-Lite. This is the newest simulated sunlight bulb available. It is more convenient than the fluorescent tube because, like the reflector flood, it can be screwed into any socket and moved around to various locations. This grow-light can be purchased for about $5 in either 75- or 100-watt sizes at your local plant, hardware, or five-and-dime store. It is an excellent form of artificial light for your plants.

Incandescent Bulb. The ordinary incandescent bulb used to light your house is the cheapest and easiest to use. Although it doesn't have some of the advantages of the other kinds, it still is a satisfactory light for your plants. There is no difference between the soft-white and the clear types. Heat is a problem with these bulbs, so follow the advice for reflector floods and keep the bulb at a good distance from the plants.

A few last words about artificial light: The heat factor is very important when arranging your lighting fixtures on the plants. If the leaves of plants become too hot, they cannot carry out the process of photosynthesis, the process by which the leaves change light to food energy. If the leaves feel warm to the touch, it means they are too hot and that the plant or the light should be moved.

As with natural light, plants in artificial light have

the characteristic of leaning or stretching toward the light source. This is called phototropism. In order to keep the natural shape of the plant, be sure to rotate the pot so all sides get light. This can be done at the end of the day with some plants like Coleus. They turn very quickly toward the light. Other plants take a few days to tilt noticeably. Rotation is not only important for shape but for proper distribution of energy-giving light.

3 DAILY CARE AND ROUTINES

WATERING

In trying to understand how to water your plants correctly, you will always get a great deal of conflicting—and confusing—advice. "Give your plants enough water, but don't overwater them," is the standard line. This statement may sound like it's telling you what to do, but ultimately it is too vague to give you any idea of the proper amount of water for your plants.

The only way a plant can be overwatered is by watering it *too often*. A plant can never be watered *too much at one time*. The best way to water a plant is to thoroughly soak the soil every time the plant is watered. This can be done in a variety of ways. For those of you with large sinks, your plants would surely enjoy an occasional soaking in the well. A bathtub is also a good place to give plants a total soak-through. Florists and greenhouse people use huge buckets and submerge their plants in them for 10 to 15 minutes. Watering depends on your facilities, but don't hesitate to soak the plants at watering time.

The easiest way to water a plant is from the top, with lukewarm water. Cold water is as great a shock to plants as it is to people. Ideally, water should be left to stand overnight at room temperature. This not only balances the temperature but makes it possible for all the impurities to sink to the bottom. But lukewarm water from the tap is sufficient. When you water from the top, be sure to watch for water to drain from the hole in the bottom. This is the only way you can be sure the water has reached all the soil in the pot. Otherwise you may only reach the top half of the pot, while the lower half remains dry. Keep watering even after the first drainage of water. It takes a good deal of water to permeate the soil. Then, to prevent root rot, spill out whatever water is left in the dish or tray underneath.

After you have followed this procedure, wait until the plant soil is bone-dry before watering again. This will decrease your chances of overwatering. Since each plant uses water at a different rate, you should feel the soil to get a signal from the plant whether to water or not. There are no rules about watering a specific plant once, twice, or three times a week. There are too many variables to have such restrictions. Just because you watered all your plants on Monday doesn't mean you do it again to all your plants again next Monday. Some of the plants will need it again on Wednesday, some on Saturday, and others not until Monday. Move the soil around with your fingers to feel whether it's moist or dry. Don't just feel the top layer either. Get right down in there. Sometimes the top part is dry as sand while the lower layers are still moist. If this is the case, then it doesn't need water. Logically, the soil on top will dry out faster than the soil lower down

All plants need water. It is simply a question of how much and how often. The only one who can really tell how much a plant needs is the person taking care of it. You can have a general idea of the way a plant needs to be watered, but the conditions of the specific environment must be taken into account. Since many homes are centrally heated or heated by radiators, the drying factor of the air must be considered. The soil will dry out faster in the living room, which is relatively dry, than it will in the bathroom, which is relatively humid. So besides the plant using water for nourishment from the soil, the air is also contributing to drying out the soil.

One sure way to combat dryness in the atmosphere around your plants is to place the pots on top of a tray of pebbles. Or, place a one-inch layer of pebbles in the dish under each plant. The water that drains out the hole in the bottom of the pot after watering will remain in this layer of stones. Gradually the water will evaporate, but the humidity from the evaporation will provide a moister atmosphere around the foliage of the plant. If the excess water from drainage gets higher than the top of the layer of pebbles, just pour it out till the water is even with the top of the pebble bed. A plant must *never* be allowed to sit in water. If it does, the roots will become soggy and rotten. If the roots drown in water, you can be sure your plants will die.

Some plants, like the asparagus fern, enjoy being moistened everyday. Others can go for weeks without water. The suggestions given in the descriptions of specific plants will be a good *guideline* for you, but be flexible. You are the one who will have to decide from observation how much water your plants need. The only way you are going to figure this out is by experimenting. If you are careful and thoughtful, you will be able to understand the signals your plants are sending you. For instance, some plant leaves go limp when they are thirsty. If leaves droop and the soil is dry, your plant needs water desperately. On the other hand, if you are overwatering a plant, the leaves will droop too, but they will usually turn yellow as well. If leaves are limp or falling but the soil is still damp, try letting the plant dry out *completely* before giving it any more water. It's better to water too little than too much.

Leaves turn brown and brittle if they are too dry. If this is happening check the soil. The clue will usually be there. Examine the symptoms and compare them with what you are doing. You should be able to decide for yourself what the proper course of action should be. If you're not sure what's happening, try the opposite treatment of the present one. Assess the situation and don't be afraid to experiment, especially in the first few weeks of taking care of a new plant. That is the time to get to know its temperament. Some leaves or even branches may fall off, the plant may thin out considerably, some leaves may yellow. Even if you really butcher a plant, you can still make it thrive, once you get the hang of its care. There's plenty of life left in a plant below the surface even when you think it's dead. *So don't throw it out!* Plants can come back from nothing. Experiencing a crisis with the care of a plant is the best and quickest way to learn for yourself the most beneficial method of watering. *Be bold!*

SPRAYING

Most plants appreciate a good misting with plain lukewarm water as often during the week as possible.

Some plants, like asparagus fern and fittonia, will only flourish when there is a high degree of moisture in the environment. They need a great deal of spraying every day to encourage growth. On the whole, plants need to be sprayed a few times a week to help them combat the dryness of most homes and offices. (This includes everything except geraniums, African violets, and begonias.)

The most convenient way to do this is to keep a spray gun filled with water sitting at room temperature at all times. Then you can just pick it up at whim and spray your grateful plants. You can buy spray guns or misters at plant shops or florists, but the cheapest solution is to use an empty plastic spray bottle from a liquid cleaner. It provides a fine, even mist perfect for plants. If the water is kept standing for at least 24 hours, all the harmful additives like fluoride will sink to the bottom. If you don't let the water stand, be sure it's lukewarm coming from the tap. The plants will not appreciate a cold mist.

The moisture the plant receives on its leaves will help it to breathe. You know how you feel in a dry room: your throat gets scratchy and you feel generally dehydrated. You would be surprised how good a fine gentle mist feels. Try it on yourself sometime. It's very refreshing.

CLEANING

People are always complaining that their plants never look as good as the ones they see in plant shops. Common descriptions of what the plants look like in the home are droopy leaves, yellow leaves, brown and shriveled leaves, and yellow or brown tips on plants like palms and spiders. People think their plants are sick when, in most cases, all that has to be done is remove decaying leaves and flowers regularly. In the natural life cycle of plants, it is inevitable that mature leaves die as new growth continues. You cannot avoid losing some leaves when you are dealing with a living plant. Just in the natural process a certain amount of yellowing, browning, and shriveling will occur, and the process cannot be reversed. No amount of care will make them green again. When that happens you might as well accept it and pick them off the plant completely. As leaves die, they drain food and energy from the rest of the plant, which is healthy and really needs the nourishment. When you take off decaying material, you will be pleasantly surprised at how healthy the plant will look. Pluck off the decayed material or snip brown tips with a scissor. All that is left to see is green, healthy matter, so that sick appearance no longer exists. If you are consistent about this practice, your plants will always look perky and very much alive. So, by doing this you are not only strengthening the plant but also keeping it from looking like it's on the way out.

Another vital aspect of cleaning your plants on a regular basis is the removal of soot or dust from the foliage. Plants breathe air and receive moisture through their foliage. If the foliage is covered with a screen of dirt, the process is inhibited.

There are two ways to handle this routine procedure. One way is to spray the foliage with a dilute solution of a mild soap such as Ivory Liquid (two drops per quart of lukewarm water). Spray freely as if you were using plain water for moisturizing. Once a week is sufficient. This solution has the added feature of protecting plants from pests and diseases—a little preventive medicine. The second way to clean foliage is to wipe the leaves gently with a damp sponge or cloth with the same solution as the spray.

Consider each plant individually when deciding whether to use the spray or wipe method. The wipe method is practical for plants with wide leaves, such as palms, rubber plants, philodendrons, nepthytis, avocados, dieffenbachia, and monstera. The spray method is better for more delicate plants or plants with more profuse foliage, such as ivies, coleus, wandering Jew, Swedish ivy, and, of course, ferns. These are not rules but suggestions. Do what you are most comfortable with. If the plant is fragile it is wiser not to wipe the leaves. If the leaves are fuzzy and furry like those of geraniums, African violets, begonias, and piggybacks, don't spray them at all. These few plants don't like water on their leaves.

It is amazing what a pick-me-up cleaning can be for a plant weighed down with soot and dust. After a good wipe and then spray with plain water there is a noticeable bounce in its stance. The wipe method only needs to be done about once a week—unless of course, you notice a plant in need.

4 TWENTY NO-HASSLE PLANTS

All the houseplants included here are sold on the market as common varieties. They have been chosen because of their merits as potential successes. They are divided into two groups. This chapter contains plants that are guaranteed not to fail unless you are very brutal or totally unaware. Chapter 6 contains plants whose care takes a little more of your time, but don't let this frighten you away. It's just helpful to know more about them to make them flourish. This does not mean you shouldn't go out and buy the plants in the second group. They work too.

No attempt is made to be comprehensive. If you happen to have a fern, begonia, or palm, for example, which is not pictured or mentioned here, don't panic. All the information can be generalized to include your specific variety. It may be worthwhile to look here before buying a new plant. In this way you can coordinate plants you might want with your conditions.

All plants are listed according to their common name or nickname. Where they differ from the common names, the Latin genus (or sometimes species) names are given parenthetically for those of you who want them.

DRACAENA

Dracaena Marginata   Dracaena Warnecki

Not only does your house have the most adverse conditions imaginable, but you don't know the first thing about how to care for a plant. In spite of this you want some plants in your house. What should you do?

For such a tall order here are some great old standbys even if you're not in as bad shape as described above. There are three species of the genus *Dracaena* available as houseplants, and each looks sufficiently different from the others that if you have only these three plants everyone will think they are from various families and that you're really a whiz with plants. Another bonus is their size, which ranges from five-inch-pot size to large trees with a couple of branches. They are exotic and attractive and don't necessarily have to be kept by a window.

The *Dracaena marginata* can be seen as decoration in museums, in offices, and generally in places where there aren't any windows—simply some kind of artificial light. They have long, thin leaves with a reddish outline and form a stalk as they mature. The more expensive varieties have long, curvy stalks that branch off in all directions, looking like a couple of miniature coconut trees you picked up in the Carribbean. This plant needs a good dunking or soaking every week or so, and that's about it. If the new growth shrivels on top, it's getting too much light, and if it gets floppy, it's not getting enough. Remember not to water it more than I've mentioned and you've got yourself a winner.

The *Dracaena warnecki* has larger, less delicate leaves than the *marginata* and distinctive coloring. The dark green leaf with white stripes down the center is perched on a thin stalk. This species is usually about three feet tall. Water this cheerful item whenever the soil is dry, usually every three or four days, depending on the humidity level of your home. It is a fast grower and will forge ahead every time it is repotted.

The *Dracaena massangeana* is potentially the largest, some growing as high as ten feet. The *massangeana*, also called the corn plant, grows on a stalk and has

Dracaena Massangeana

multiple branches. The leaf is more than a foot long
and lightly colored, with a yellow interior and dark
green edges. Sometimes the coloring tends toward
light green inside, not giving it as varied a quality as
you might like, so keep that in mind when choosing
one at the store.

The *massangeana* grows in spurts between long
periods of dormancy. Don't get discouraged. When it
finally does grow, it's great to watch each new leaf
add height and dimension to the plant. There is some-

thing very luxurious about the graceful hanging of the huge leaves and the general perkiness of the plant as a whole. Remember to wipe the long leaves with a damp cloth or sponge once a week to remove dust and soot; it will maintain the health of the plant and keep the leaves naturally glossy. That goes for the *warnecki*, too; but leave the *marginata* leaves alone, because they are more delicate and don't like to be touched. The plant man I bought my *marginata* from many years ago said I shouldn't touch the leaves because they would die. Mine eventually did die but I couldn't swear that was the reason.

Water the *massangeana* when the soil is dry— probably every five or six days, again depending on how dry your house is. You should have no problem with any of these dracaenas, especially since they are not prone to pests. If the tips of the leaves turn brown, snip them off to a point, so a blunt edge isn't noticeable among the other leaves. They all like a good spray once or twice a week and propagate by air-layering.

PHILODENDRON

Philodendron—the ideal houseplant. If you took a hatchet and lopped off a few vines of any philodendron, not only wouldn't you kill it, but more shoots would appear in no time to replace those lost. There are hundreds of species, all of which will thrive under the most adverse conditions. They need practically no light, may be watered haphazardly, and don't mind dry air— unless they're sitting on top of the radiator. This, of course, is an exaggeration of an extreme condition. If

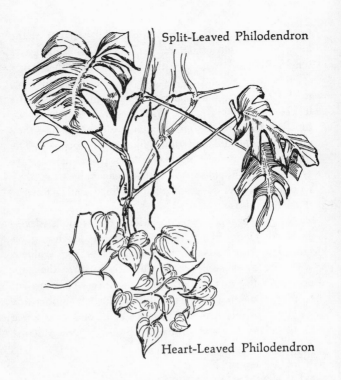

Split-Leaved Philodendron

Heart-Leaved Philodendron

any extra care is given to them, they will practically take over the room. Very little light (natural or artificial) and a good soaking when the soil is dry is all that is necessary to make them grow like crazy.

The enormous genus *Philodendron* is made up of climbers. (A climber is a vine that creeps along the ground using its aerial roots to attach itself to moist ground or to moist tree branches; it can be successfully grown in water as well as soil.) There are so many hybrid versions that only the most common houseplant varieties can be included here. The most popular and graceful is the heart-leaved philodendron, which looks exactly like what its name implies. The leaves are generally small, ranging generally from three to six inches, depending, on whether it is growing upward along a support or not. Philodendrons can either be trained to climb a support, such as a slab of moist peat moss or bark or a dry garden support. The size of the leaf usually increases when the vine is allowed to climb. Otherwise you can allow the vine to cascade from a hanging pot or from a regular pot placed high enough to give the foliage room to drop.

Some other varieties of philodendron are the spear-leaved philodendron and the split-leaved philodendron. Both types are longer and larger than the heart-leaved and look as if someone had taken a scissor and cut out parts of the smooth, glossy leaf, making it irregularly shaped.

Philodendrons may be kept in dark locations of your home or office, but they would welcome light, artificial or natural, at some point during the day. Even plants that have a reputation for doing well in the dark will do even better with the benefit of a little light. With a minimum amount of light, these plants will grow indefinitely, with hardly any leaf loss. This will result in fabulously bushy and heavy growth. I had my heart-leaved philodendrons in a very dark corner of the room for a few weeks when I first bought them and never gave them extra light. Soon they sagged and drooped, looking generally pathetic. Some browning and yellowing occurred, and they didn't grow. I switched them to the window, and now they are going berserk. They don't *have* to have light, but they like it.

The frequency of watering determines the rate of growth. If you want to suppress the growth for decorative reasons, let the soil go dry before watering again. Otherwise, the soil may be kept evenly moist for faster growth. Any time that *any* part of a vine gets yellow or sickly looking, simply cut that part off. Everytime I have done this, more growth has popped right up within a couple of weeks, making the entire plant healthier and stronger.

All philodendrons are solid green, without pattern or muted coloration. Their beauty lies not in exotic markings but in their strength and fortitude. Philodendrons can easily be propagated by stem cuttings or pinning and winding to wet soil or vermiculite so that the aerial roots will erupt.

CAST-IRON PLANT
(*Aspidistra*)

Cast-Iron Plant

26

Commonly known as the cast-iron plant, the aspidistra will tolerate the very worst conditions and still grow. It is stemless and has long, slender green leaves that grow from the center of the plant, directly up from the soil. It is native to China—if that's any incentive to buy one. Besides the dark green leaf, there is a variegated green-and-white-striped kind, which, however, needs more light than the former.

The leaves of the aspidistra will crack if it's not getting enough water, but otherwise, it tolerates dark corners, drafts, low temperatures (not below freezing), and the absence of sunlight. Brownish purple flowers sometimes appear at the base of the plant if it is being treated well. If it grows under such poor conditions, you can imagine what happens to it with a fair amount of light and a little warmth and attention.

FALSE ARALIA
(Dizygotheca)

The false aralia is an upright growing shrub whose stem is barklike, reaching up to five feet. The leaves are leathery copper-colored projections like ultraskinny fingers. It has a spindly, airy quality that makes a good contrast with more thickly foliated houseplants. It can lose its lower leaves easily but will remain looking well. Keep the soil moist at all times and give it bright light. It even likes a few hours of sunlight. If it's not getting enough light and humidity, it will get "leggy," but there is no way to make it bushier except by cutting back the main stem in the summer.

False Aralia

The aralia will still look interesting since its long leaves (up to 10 inches) create an eerie, even bizarre, effect. Stem cuttings of the false aralia can be rooted and will grow to the height of 10 feet in three years. Spray it liberally with water, keep it away from drafts, and you won't have much to worry about.

SUCCULENTS

The succulents (a descriptive term, not a formal classification) comprise a wide range of plants aside from cacti (here discussed separately). Succulents offer enough variety so that an entire plant collection can be made up of only succulents and still be interesting and diverse. Generally, succulents require bright light or direct sun, cool rooms, and very little water. They have fleshy, waxy, very thick leaves that can store water for long periods of drought. Usually two weeks can go by without watering, and maybe more, unless your room is very dry. The only way to tell whether it needs watering is by feeling the soil. If it's dry and hard or sandlike, it needs water. Succulents need a great deal of sun or bright light, but during the summer months, direct sun is too hot and will burn the foliage, causing browning and withering.

These "spineless cacti" are incredibly delicate in form and color. They grow in a variety of rosettes, sometimes scalloped at the edges or cup-shaped like rosebuds in bloom. They are all softly textured and smooth and delicate to the touch. Some even have a slightly furry coating. They are as sensitive as they look and become easily bruised when not handled gently. Their colorings are the most provocative and sumptuous pastels I've ever seen on plants. Many have smoky hues of pale yellow, grey-green, sea green, ivory, lavender, and mottled darker greens. A wonderful decorative possibility open to you with succulents is to plant many different kinds together in one pot or dish. The arrangment can be any that you want but will always be lush, overflowing, and extravagant.

When you touch their growth you'll want to squeeze, but don't do it—all the water stored in the tissue will come oozing out. This will damage the plant, causing that area to brown, even die. The following is a list of succulents you can grow with great success and a minimum of care. All of them grow much

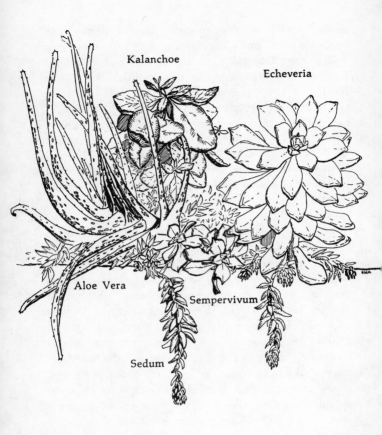

Kalanchoe

Echeveria

Aloe Vera

Sempervivum

Sedum

faster than cacti and are therefore more rewarding for those who need more immediate reinforcement for their efforts. There are many different species to choose from within each of the five genera.

SEDUM. There are many species of sedums. They are unusually chunky, voluptuous leaves that look like points growing around thick stems. Some are vine-like, others grow like shrubs. They are delicate and brittle, falling off at various points, causing frustration to the owner. The best thing about a sedum, compared with other hanging-vine-like plants, is that it retains mature leaves, thereby keeping itself fat and full, no pinching required (see chapter 5). Even though sedum's break from the slighest touch, they root without any problem whatsoever. Donkey-Tail, or Burro's-Tail, sedum has chains of waxy blue-green leaves. To prevent breakage, it is best grown in a hanging pot away from any traffic in the room. *Sedum Mexicana* is less chunky, but has the same appearance. It also grows very quickly and easily, stretching its branches toward the light.

ECHEVERIAS. The echeverias grow in a cuplike rosebud formation designed to catch any water that might be coming their way, to send down to their roots. The more light they receive, the deeper their breathtaking pastels will become. There are echeverias that sprout tiny offsets (plantlets), which remain attached to the mother plant, creating a larger and fuller effect for the plant. Echeverias, often used as ground covers in gardens, produce spikes of brightly colored blossoms. These succulents can be propagated by leaf cuttings rooted in a growing medium, and by cutting back a leaf you can stimulate new growth.

ALOES. Aloes look more like cacti in their irregular, pointy, and jagged formations. But aloes are smooth, soft, and waxy. They contain a soothing gel that is used as a skin moisturizer, and is one of the best kitchen burn and sunburn relievers—many people keep them just for that purpose. Aloes, being heavy, tend to lean over easily on the rim of the pot. This may bruise the outer leaves, turning them brown and flattening them. Just cut off those leaves at their base, since aloes grow quickly to make up for this loss. They are difficult to propagate, but some send out offsets.

KALANCHOES. Kalanchoes, which originate in Madagascar, are, unlike the other succulents, appreciated more for their leafy quality and red-orange blossoms than for the desert effect. They are shrubby in shape, with clusters of thick leaves. They take more water than the others and should be shielded from bright, direct sun in the summertime.

SEMPERVIVUMS. These are the hardiest rosette succulent plants. They need scarcely any water and tolerate poorer conditions than the other succulents. Most have pale green leaves edged in red-brown. They are easiest to grow in shallow dishes and pans. They multiply by spreading offsets right next to the mother plant. They still need a great deal of light like the others, so don't take advantage of their good nature.

CACTI

Cacti are the standbys for people who go away a great deal and must leave their plants alone or for those who stay home a great deal and don't want to be bothered with more than a good soaking infrequently. Cacti, being succulents, store water in their

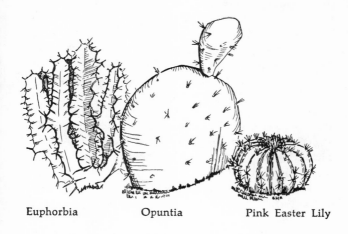

Euphorbia   Opuntia   Pink Easter Lily

leaves, enabling them to go for weeks without water. But cacti need even less water than other succulents. They come in thousands of varieties, each having a more bizarre and exciting form than the next.

All cacti have an intricate network of prickles and thorns that can cause extraordinary pain if they become embedded in your fingers. These are nature's protective devices to ward off animals and humans from getting to the water inside. Since cacti are so fascinating, usually your first instinct is to reach out and touch. Watch out! The pain can last for days, and the thorns are practically impossible to remove.

Cacti often come in tiny pots and look very delicate, although squat. They can also be bought at very high prices in huge tubs. These trees range from four to seven feet high, just like the ones out on the range.

Their unique shapes and configurations lend humor to your fantasy life and will be a great conversation piece in your home—if that's what you want. All this and flowers too if you are patient and give your cactus a lot of sun. Hot and dry houses are similar to their natural environment, so there is no problem there. But blossoms will develop only if the cactus is placed in a cool place during the winter.

Cacti do best in plastic pots, which help preserve the water supply. If your cactus looks sickly or shriveled, you are probably overwatering it. The first cactus I ever had just collapsed one day in a sea of mush like a burst water balloon. Obviously, it had suffered from a modern day equivalent of Chinese water torture. Once every month or so, water your cactus. Since they are very slow growers, cacti don't need repotting very often—every three years or so. When you do repot a cactus, use heavy oven mitts to avoid thorns.

One last word—I once heard of someone who watered his cacti whenever it rained in what he thought was their native environment. He checked the newspaper every day for the weather conditions in New Mexico and Arizona. If it rained there he watered his cacti. I doubt that this is sound advice. Remember, the less water cacti receive, the better off they are. This cannot be emphasized strongly enough. Lots of sun is important to keep up their irregular and un-usual shapes. Don't stick them off in a corner just because they don't demand as much attention and care as foliage plants.

Opuntias are the most common and hardiest variety. Their identifying characteristics are relatively few thorns, flat bodies, and ear-like protuberances. Christmas cacti and Thanksgiving cacti put forth beautiful flowers at those times of year, but they don't have that desert quality of the more heavily thorned species.

Arrange small cacti in a dish together in part sand and part regular potting soil. It will look stupendous. Enjoy them—they're such easygoing plants.

COLUMNEA

Columnea

If you don't have much light but can provide any form of artificial light, columnea will grow into a magnificent hanging, trailing evergreen that will flower easily, with large red, luscious, lillylike flowers. The leaves, which are shiny, waxy dark green, have a thick, succulent quality. It sounds unbelievable, but you can make it happen.

If you provide either a great deal of artificial light or a lot of sunlight, columnea will dry out quickly, so remember to spray it often with plain water. Spraying twice a day will make it very happy, but let the soil dry out before watering again.

The key to blossoms is coolness, so keep the columnea near, or in, the window, especially during the winter, to encourage blooms. Spraying with cold water is also a help, so no matter what, don't forget to mist your columnea often. The columnea is difficult to propagate except in greenhouse conditions but is so hardy that it will not thin out as other vinelike plants do. If you want to try propagating it, do it by rooting tip cuttings.

PRAYER PLANT
(Maranta)

During the day, the leaves of the prayer plant fall every which way, whether it is hanging down low or growing upward on a guide stick, but after dark, they stand straight up, stretching toward the sky. It is then that they display their rich burgandy undersides.

There are two species of Maranta. The Maranta

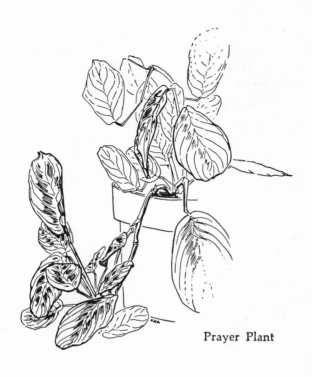

Prayer Plant

kerchveana is small, thin, and delicate. It is a very pale green with brownish blotches arranged in a double row. The veins on the leaf are barely distinguishable on this species. The other is called *Maranta massangeana* (not to be confused with *Dracaena massangeana*). It has a much more intricate and pronounced pattern on its leaf. The background is a deep bottle green shaded with a lighter and brighter green, which creates a spotted effect. The colors in this type are much more vibrant than those of the *kerchveana*, but if you see the two species together, you will know they are from the same family. The *massangeana* has a vein configuration etched in fire-engine red, adding to the unusual color and design of this very uncommon common houseplant. The leaves reproduce by unfurling from the ones that came before them. As they mature, their pattern and color become more distinct.

The prayer plant can be either trained upward on a stick or allowed to hang free to drop downward like a creeper. It grows quickly and abundantly with enough humidity. Ideally, the prayer plant needs greenhouse or terrarium conditions. Spray it a few times a week with plain lukewarm water to provide the extra moisture. Also, try placing the pot on top of a layer of pebbles and water (see chapter 3). Keep the prayer plant moist at all times except in the winter, when its growth cycle slows down. Then, water when the soil dries out. The prayer plant likes light, but very bright light or sunlight will bleach out its lovely colors. Partial shade is not harmful either, as long as there's some extra artificial or natural light given the plant a few times a week. As you might have guessed from its description, the prayer plant does unbelievably well in terrariums, which offer high humidity, warmth, adequate light, and just the right amount of water.

One last item. I noticed that during the summer small runners pop out from all over my *Maranta massangeana*. I had no idea what they were for, so I decided to leave them alone, expecting that something might happen. Sure enough, soon the runners opened at their tips into delicate, tiny flowers. They were white, with deep violet centers. The entire flower was barely the size of my fingertip. The process, from budding to full bloom, lasted about three days, and each flower lasted a day or two. In all, about six or eight flowers emerged in one month. I didn't even know the prayer plant flowered when I bought it, so it was a real thrill.

Marantas are very easy plants to take care of and grow to be bushy and strong. Don't leave them in a draft—their leaves will turn yellow at the tips. Propagate marantas by division.

UMBRELLA TREE
(Schefflera)

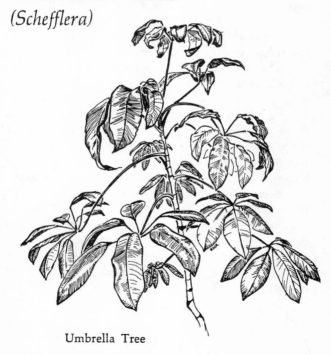

Umbrella Tree

Nicknamed the Australian umbrella tree, since it comes from the rain forests of Australia, the schefflera combines impressiveness of appearance and size with ease of care and handling. They are sold in the United States in many different sizes. Some come in small pots as seedlings, while others are expensive 12-foot specimens. Each large leaf is made up of about four or five leaflets, all arising from a central point and looking like fingers. On the larger trees these leaves could probably shelter anyone from a rain shower. The leaves are dark green, with a glossy surface. Make sure to wipe the surfaces of all the leaves often, to maintain their shine and remove all soot and dust.

The nice thing about schefflera is that it will take bright light or direct sun. They will also survive where the light is dim, but I wouldn't recommend it. Heat and moisture make these plants grow quickly, but if your house is dry it can also withstand that condition. They simply won't grow as quickly. Give it extra misting if your house is unusually dry. Pebbles under the pot won't hurt either. Soak the soil thoroughly when watering and then let it dry out completely until the surface soil is sandy before watering again. Schefflera will live for years in the same pot, so don't be anxious to repot it.

Schefflera is a no-hassle plant if you make sure it doesn't get pests. Spider mites and mealy bugs are attracted to this plant, so be conscientious about cleaning the leaves with a soap and water solution (see chapter 5).

VELVET PLANT
(Gynura)

Velvet Plant

When I first discovered this plant it was called a purple passion plant. Since then I have heard it called velvet plant or purple Java plant. But its official common name is velvet plant. Usually the name conjures up the exotic quality of jungle foliage. Deep violet hairs grow all over the plant giving it a very fuzzy appearance. It's the kind of plant you want to touch as soon as you see it. The leaves are pine green and covered with purple hairs, as are the stems. It grows like a vine, making it a good trailing plant for hanging pots or regular pots placed up high so that the fast-growing vines have room to cascade. I've seen velvet plants grow up to four feet long, but unless they are pinched often, they won't branch out to create new growth. If left to their own devices they will lose leaves and become weak, so pinch continuously. They grow incredibly fast, demanding only one thing constantly: lots and lots of water. The velvet plant will droop or go totally limp from lack of water. That's how you know when its thirsty Its symptoms are unmistakable. Watering will return its shape immediately or within hours if it's been left without water for more than a day. Sometimes in dry apartments this plant needs watering twice a day. The oval leaves have a strange odor, and mature plants sometimes blossom with gold-orange flowers in the fall. Spray often with plain water since gynura likes moisture and be sure to give it plenty of light. Pebbles in a dish beneath will also provide extra moisture. Sunlight isn't necessary, but the greater amount of light, the deeper and richer the coloration. Sunlight creates too much heat for the velvet plant, which likes cool places and lots of moisture. Propagate the velvet plant by stem cuttings rooted in mediums of peat moss or sand.

SPATHIPHYLLUM

Here's a plant for dark homes and offices or novice gardeners, since success is almost guaranteed. Rooms heated by steam radiators, which create a very dry heat, won't faze it either. The spathiphyllum is related to another plant you may own already if your conditions match the ones I've just described—the philodendron, another plant that never says die. There is only one catch to this terrifically hardy plant: the spathiphyllum needs lots of water. Just because it's so tolerant of poor environments doesn't mean you

Spathiphyllum

1 DON'T BE AFRAID OF YOUR PLANTS

This book is for people who don't understand plant books. It's not a manual or garden textbook. If you like plants and want to start a collection, or if you already have plants but need a little help understanding what they're all about, this book is for you. The most important thing to know before you begin is that plants have no secrets. *They* will tell you all you need to know to keep them healthy and happy. It is up to you to understand their way of communicating. When you get over the idea that there is too much technical information for you to grasp before you can be a successful plant grower, you are over the hump.

You can have a plant collection that will not control your life but rather give you a great amount of pleasure. Plants can become like friends, each having its own personality once you get to know it. You don't have to become a slave to your plants for them to thrive, but you do have to observe what's happening with them in order to give the little push they need to get along. Nothing you have to do is difficult or complicated. It's all common sense and simply a question of familiarizing yourself with each plant. Above all, remember that there's a lot of life in every plant— don't be afraid that touching it too harshly will cause it to keel over and die. Plants have a resilient quality that guarantees a comeback no matter how you think you've butchered them.

can forget about daily watering. There aren't many plants I would water every day, but if you don't give this one a daily dose of water it will keel over right before your eyes. It will revive immediately after watering if it hasn't been left for too long a period without water. Otherwise, it may take longer.

It is very important to give the spathiphyllum roots a constant water supply. A plastic pot is one good solution to this problem of water retention. The spathiphyllum grows best in a window with no sun, but will also grow well with practically no light at all. The spathiphyllum hates sun, even a small amount, so keep it out of southern exposures. If it's given light, you will probably be treated to small white blossoms that last a long time and look like lilies. As with the maranta flower, when it dies, cut it off at the base of its stem.

The spathiphyllum comes with either large or small leaves, which grow quickly from the crown of the plant. They can be divided easily, and you'll find yourself with a new plant or two. You can also pot a few together and come up with quite a voluptuous plant. It does need humidity, so spray it or keep it on a bed of pebbles to retain the moisture from watering. You can't go wrong with this easy-to-grow plant. Besides, it's more interesting looking than some others that are as hard to kill.

SANSEVIERIA

Sansevieria, including Hahn's plant and the snake plant, is the kind of plant that you can practically for

Snake Plant Hahn's Plant

get about because its so tough. It does not need much
light and will grow well in a dark area of the room.
It doesn't grow very fast, but it grows steadily. A
sansevieria is a stable, enduring addition to your plant
collection. If you have had trouble keeping more delicate plants alive, this is the plant for you. The only

way you could possibly fail with these hardy thick-leaved plants is to overwater them. That too would be quite difficult because they like dry soil and can be watered once a week, sometimes less. Most sansevierias will not need repotting for several years because the roots grow slowly and enjoy the confinement of a pot.

The Hahn's variety has leaves four to six inches long that grow outward from the center in a rosette. The dark green with pale green leaves curve over the edge of the pot, giving the plant the look of a lush summer flower, with a pale yellow new leaf peering out from the center. Each Hahn's rosette has short roots attached to its center clump. If there are several rosettes in one pot, you can separate them by division, making a pot with each rosette.

The snake plant looks quite different. It too has succulentlike leaves that grow from a rosette center. The leaves are sword-shaped, growing vertically. This species is often planted in a shallow pot or dish to contrast its straight up-and-down appearance. Snake plants look like tall, fancy-colored grass stiffly reaching for the sky. Most snake-plant leaves are mottled with greyish white or have a yellow zigzag pattern. Like the Hahn's sansevieria, the snake plant needs little light and water.

Both varieties can be propagated by leaf cuttings. Cut one leaf off the main plant. Then cut that leaf into a few sections. Each section can be set in moist sand about half an inch deep. The cutting will grow roots in the sand and a new cluster of foliage on the top. It can then be planted in soil.

All species of sansevieria are excellent plants for the kitchen, as they can tolerate any gas that might leak from the stove.

46

PEPEROMIA

Emerald Ripple Peperomia

Watermelon Peperomia   Blunt-Leaved Peperomia

Peperomia is the perfect plant for someone who is willing to water it, but do almost nothing else. All varieties are very easy to care for and need only a little of your time. They require medium light and often can be used decoratively on tables because they are low-growing bushy plants. They should be watered when the soil is almost completely dry, but be careful because they overwater quite readily. Peperomias rarely grow larger than a foot, so you probably won't ever have to repot them. They do not need to be pinched, as they stay compact and bushy on their own.

Most varieties of peperomia have leaves one to four inches long growing on fleshy red-green stems. They all grow flower stalks in the spring that look like mouse tails. The most popular varieties are the watermelon, the emerald ripple, and the blunt-leaved peperomias.

The watermelon peperomia has heart-shaped dark green leaves with white stripes moving outward symmetrically from the center. There is one leaf at the end of each stem, thus the larger the plant, the larger the cluster of stems.

The emerald ripple develops in the same clustered way as the watermelon variety. It too has reddish stems with one heart-shaped leaf at the top. These leaves however, are all dark green and wrinkled. On close inspection the wrinkles look like a series of steep mountains and deep valleys. The leaf is quite stiff, and bending it against the grain of the wrinkles will cause it to break. This rippled effect makes the plant fun to look at. Because there are so many varied surfaces, be sure to spray the leaves often so that they don't collect a lot of dirt.

The blunt-leaved peperomia, either plain or variegated, is quite different from the other kinds. It has somewhat larger, roundish leaves. They are smooth and shiny. They are dark green, sometimes having blotches of white and pale green. Because the leaves are quite heavy and all attached to one stem, the stem often tends to curve according to the leaf distribution. If trained, the blunt-leaved peperomia can be used as a hanging plant.

All peperomias can be easily propagated from stem cuttings. Don't worry when you put a cutting in the rooting medium if it takes a very long time to develop roots. The cutting will remain healthy and should show roots in three to six weeks.

SPIDER PLANT
(Chlorophytum)

Spider Plant

Spider plants are easy to care for and extremely hardy. They have a tropical appearance that will add a jungle-like quality to a room, especially when planted in a hanging pot. The thick foliage, which grows directly from the soil, resembles a thin dracaena leaf, lightly colored in green and white. Out from the center of this growth come long shoots called runners. These grow to approximately two feet. From the long runners sprout smaller runners with offsets, or miniature versions of the mother plant. Each runner has anywhere from one to four offsets, depending on how old the plant is. Because of their spread, spider plants are usually sold in hanging pots.

Don't overwater these plants or else the leaves will turn yellow and go limp. Soak the soil thoroughly and then let it dry out completely before watering again. The palmlike leaves grow very close together in thick clusters. Because of crowding, it is normal for the leaves to push into one another, causing breakage or bending. Anytime a leaf is injured in this way, it will brown at the sensitive area. Don't worry about this. It is the plant and not you. Simply cut the leaf diagonally to make a point at the end. This helps to retain its natural shape rather than giving the leaf a blunt edge. Only if there is browning or yellowing throughout the plant does it mean you are overwatering it.

Spider plants will do well in filtered light. They also appreciate a good spray once or twice a week with plain water.

Spider plants are fun and easy to propagate. Cut the runner directly above the offset you have chosen to root. It doesn't really matter exactly where you cut, since once it is rooted, the runner can be cut off completely. Fill a small pot with soil, and place the offset right on top. Stick a straight pin directly through the center of the offset down into the soil. This will keep it firmly planted to the soil to facilitate root growth. Then soak the soil thoroughly until water comes out the bottom hole. Keep the soil very wet even if it means watering it every day. At this stage in its rooting process it needs as much moisture as possible. It may go limp at first, but give it a couple of weeks and it should root and grow quickly. You can even put more than one miniature in a pot, creating a larger plant and a greater possibility of success. Some may go into shock and never come back. If an offset is still limp after two weeks, throw it out and try again.

Spider plants can also be propagated by dividing the mother plant (see "Division" in chapter 7).

MARBLE QUEEN
(Scindapsus)

Here's another plant for all of you with dark apartments. It is also a sure thing for novice gardeners who don't yet have faith in themselves. The marble queen, also called devil's ivy and pothos, is a creeper. It will grow forever to tremendous lengths on one stem. In one pot there are usually two or three trailing vines, which become ungainly and leave the top somewhat bare unless you have a voluminously planted pot filled with growing stems. There are several things you can do about this situation. As with the other creepers, marble queen can be guided by string, sticks, or pieces of bark to grow upward along windows and walls. It

Marble Queen

is said that forcing the growth of creepers upward increases the leaf size too—sometimes up to two feet long. Or, you can let the marble queen trail down and, as the plant matures, take some of the vines and wind and pin them on top of the soil (see "Winding and Pinning" in chapter 7). Make sure to crush the stems slightly and to keep the soil moist. Within a few days new roots should appear, making the plant stronger and creating new growth on top, where it needs it.

These are incredibly hardy plants that anybody can grow. They can remain in the same pot for over a year eliminating the transplanting process for beginners until they are ready and have become comfortable with their plants. Marble queen is also one of the few plants that can be grown forever in only water. They are very attractive and just as healthy when raised in a large, moderately shallow bowl of water. I have seen them arranged this way in fountains, too, looking very tropical and lush. The leaf is heart-shaped, with distinctive variations in color. Some are splashed with white and green; others, green and yellow. Abundant light will make their colorings more vivid but isn't necessary for growth. Normally they should be allowed to dry out before watering and can be cut back without fear, because pruning encourages new growth. Propagate by division, leaf cuttings, or stem cuttings (see chapter 7).

DUMB CANE
(Dieffenbachia)

Dieffenbachia, or dumb cane, is an extremely hardy plant that is easy to grow in the home environment. The massive leaves give the dieffenbachia a grandeur and regal distinction all its own. Even when young, with few leaves, this plant commands a large space and a feeling of junglelike fullness.

The leaves are 6–18 inches long and 4–8 inches wide.

Dumb Cane

They usually have light green and white irregular blotches stemming from the central rib with a very dark green edging. The plant itself can be from 2½ to 5½ feet tall at maturity. The lower leaves of dieffenbachia will eventually wither in the natural growth process as new ones develop at the top. These dead leaves should be cut off and thrown away. Since both the leaves and

54

stems are poisonous, be careful that young children and pets can't get a hold of the discarded leaves. Calcium oxalate, the poison contained in the plant, causes swelling of the tongue.

Dieffenbachia needs very little care. It grows well in filtered light and should be watered when the soil is dry. This plant responds immediately to overwatering by having a leaf become limp and yellow. When this happens, let the soil dry out completely before you water again. Because the leaves are so large, they tend to collect a lot of dust and dirt. It is important to spray and sponge the leaves often so the plant can breathe properly.

Propagate dieffenbachia by air-layering and then make additional cuttings of the canelike stem.

ALUMINUM PLANT
(Pilea)

Aluminum plants grow like wildfire. They are hardy, untemperamental, and terrific to look at. This is quite a recommendation for such an inexpensive plant: it sells at almost any five-and-ten for under a dollar. Don't be deceived by a scrawny appearance in the tiny white plastic pots they come in. Transplant it after a couple of weeks adjustment in your home to a larger pot and then watch it take off. You can't miss identifying this plant because the name is so perfect. The three- to four-inch leaves are green, with a symmetrical vein-like pattern on their leaves in what could only be termed aluminum. It could almost be called iridescent.

Aluminum Plant

The silvery brushstrokes on the common oval-shaped leaf make for an unusual looking plant but one that is easy to care for with great success. I have found that pinching isn't really necessary, since the plant stays bushy without it. The leaves low on the stem don't drop off like coleus as new growth takes place, so the aluminum plant doesn't get leggy. New growth from the soil can be stimulated with pinching but will also happen without pinching. The aluminum plant likes a great deal of water. Like the zebra plant and the coleus it will wilt and look tired when it wants more water. The water provides turgidity in the stem and leaves. Another quality the aluminum plant has in common with the coleus is its degree of phototropism. The aluminum turns its leaves toward the light making the entire plant face in that direction in just a few days (the coleus does this in one day). When this happens you get the pleasure of turning the aluminum plant around to get dazzled by its sparkling leaves all facing in your direction. They will look as if you had been feeding them "super-food" to get them to look so luminous. Propagate by leaf cuttings or stem cuttings, and keep repotting this fast-growing plant to give it enough space to germinate itself.

MONSTERA
(*Monstera deliciosa*)

Monstera

Monstera plants are also called Swiss cheese plants or mistakenly labeled the split-leaf philodendron. The giant oval or circular leaves grow to well over a foot long when mature. They look very much like part of the *Philodendron* genus and are cared for in the same way. The monstera is appreciated by home horticulturalists, especially beginners, for the same hardiness, vigor, and tenacity shown by philodendrons. It is difficult to lose a strong-willed monstera already in full growth. If it is a weak young seedling, I can't make any promises. But, this is another "can't miss" plant for those of you with dimly lit apartments or offices, with fluctuating temperatures of very hot to very cold, very dry to very damp. The monstera will also withstand the sloppy and inconsistent watering habits of its owner. But I hope that no plant of yours will receive such horrendous care. With a little extra love and attention, the ones that demand less will end up giving you more.

The reason the monstera is confused with the philodendron is that when the leaves are young, they aren't perforated or lobed, as they are when they are mature. The monstera's glossy leaves are the same dark green, although having a much lighter tone when newly unfurled. Some people don't like monsteras or the large split-leaf philodendron precisely because they have that waxy, polished look. They look almost too good to be true. If you are taking the time to care for a living plant, you don't want it to look like plastic foliage. But they are huge and impressive and need not look fake.

Monsteras, like philodendrons, are vines and grow the same aerial roots that either drop down to the soil and take root, propagating the plant, or cling to slabs of moistened bark or moss for support. Monstera will grow to ceiling height with the minimum of light but will become straggly without cutting back or an aid to guide its growth. Propagation is very simple when done from stem cuttings, pinning and winding, or air-layering, depending on the size and dimension of your plant. The monstera is capable of tremendous growth but will move ahead slowly if it's living under minimal conditions. A little extra care will make it grow wildly. If you forget about it, it will still hold on.

NEPTHYTIS
(Syngonium)

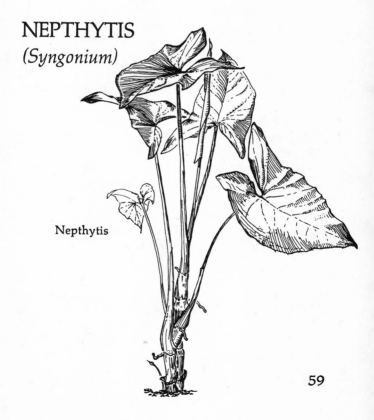

Nepthytis

If you live in a dark apartment and you think you don't have enough light to grow plants, then this is the one for you. This plant, along with philodendron, devil's ivy, and dracaena, can be grown under the most adverse conditions. Nepthytis never gives up. I had one that grew in semidarkness for two years, so there really are plants for all environments.

Nepthytis leaves look like arrowheads. Some are longer and narrower than others. Some are pointed and range from about three inches to eight inches, depending on how you grow them. If they are propped up on some sort of trellis or with a string and stick, their leaf size will increase. If you let them hang without support or guidance, they tend to become straggly. A new leaf can be observed unfolding from the stem of the previous leaf. These leaves vary in color. Some leaves are all green, while others are marked with combinations of various shades of green with cream or white.

Nepthytis does best when its soil is kept moist, but I have often allowed the soil to dry out yet the plant remained healthy. This is a good thing for new gardeners, who often forget to water plants for days on end. Nepthytis does well if you wind and pin it to the soil. This will force growth of new roots and encourage dormant shoots. Nepthytis can look tremendously bushy or look like a creeper along walls and window frames. It is a real basic.

PALM

Palms conjure up the tropics, Humphrey Bogart movies, fans on the ceiling, and mystery right around the other side of the palm. Actually, there's nothing mysterious at all about the care and maintenance of any palm. They are easy to keep, looking lush and full in all their variety of types and sizes. No palm needs direct sun but rather thrives in filtered light or partial shade. If they get too much sun, their rich green fades to a dull greenish yellow. If you have a shady corner to put one in, remember to keep an artificial light

Sentry Palm

source on the palm for a few hours a day. The small palms sold for table size will never grow to be large trees, no matter how long they live, while the huge trees will remain so with a minimum amount of attention.

Since the palm is indigenous to tropical locations, it will need a high degree of humidity around its foliage at all times. It is best to have a layer of pebbles in the tray the pot rests in, to provide moisture from evaporation. Try spraying the fronds (leaves) a few times a week, if not every day, if your room is especially dry. This additional moisture will insure the tropical deep green of the palm. I left my parlor palm near the steam-heat radiator, and in a few weeks the leaves had dried out to a shadow of their natural color. A palm needs warmth but with moisture, not dryness. Palms enjoy being kept evenly moist in their soil at all times. If there is any doubt about whether you are overwatering your palm, then let the soil go almost dry before watering again. It is better to keep it on the dry side rather than overwater it and rot the roots. Keep the foliage of palms wiped clean or sprayed with an Ivory Liquid solution (see "Cleaning" in chapter 3) to help maintain a fresh and bouncy quality to the fronds. The older fronds often yellow, especially if there is a fair amount of new growth emerging. Don't be afraid to cut these off, because they will not turn green again. If the tips of the fronds turn yellow or brown, do the same. This will keep the plant looking clean and healthy, while strengthening it.

For your identification purposes and general information, there are two basic groups of palms. Most palms sold as houseplants have leaves either fan-shaped, like the Chinese-fan palm, or feathery, like the

Chinese Fan Palm

parlor palm or butterfly palm. Distinctions between the palms within these two groups are very slight, so unless you are a palm freak, it really isn't necessary to know the exact difference. All of them need basically the same care, so there is no need to fret over their Latin names . . . unless you want to.

All palms grow from clusters of brown, fiber-covered stems. New leaves emerge from these stems, looking at first, like a tall, thin pointed bud. As the bud matures, the leaf unfurls slowly. The young leaf is lighter in color than the fully matured leaf. Some palms have fronds that swoop down gracefully in all directions like the Chinese-fan palms (the ones used by the slaves in old movies to fan Egyptian pharoahs). Others, like the butterfly, sentry, and parlor palms, look more like feathers and stand more erect. The parlor and butterfly palms may resemble one another in their leaf configuration, but when it comes to size, their similarity ends. Butterfly palms may grow as tall as 25 feet, although the houseplant variety runs more in the 12-foot category. Parlor palms rarely grow over 3 feet in the home. Palms rarely need to be repotted, but they can be propagated by division if you want to make two plants out of one. Easy going and beautiful . . . what more can one ask?

5 KEEPING YOUR PLANTS GOING ONCE THEY'VE GOTTEN STARTED

PINCHING

Pinching your plants is a very basic process that, if understood from the outset, will help you maintain strong, bushy plants. Consistent and diligent pinching is a must if you want to prevent bare-looking stems, with visible new growth only at the tip of the stem. Vinelike plants such as wandering Jew and the ivies all need to be pinched constantly so that the stem part near the soil doesn't thin out and become straggly. Then the plant looks bottom-heavy, with all its new growth at the tips of the vines. Plants that stand upright, like coleus, begonias, geraniums, and aluminum, jade, and zebra plants, all need pinching too. If they don't get it, the base of the stem keeps losing leaves, never giving off new growth below but only on top.

Most plants *must* be pinched on a regular basis in order to force the energy growth upward from the base, rather than the tip. This will not only suppress top growth and send energy downward to fill out the thinned-out stem, but for every pair of leaves that is nipped in the bud, you will gain another pair. You will double the new growth on top besides stimulating dormant buds below. There is growth lying in wait all over the plant. It just needs a little push from you to help it burst forth. You provide this encouragement by pinching the bud or tiniest leaves at the tip of the newest growth wherever it may be on your plant. There are certain plants that don't need to be pinched. Their growth patterns will not be helped by pinching. These plants are palms, dracaenas, spider plants, succulents, marantas, and, obviously, cactus. These plants don't have a great deal of leaf loss and can take care of themselves. You can usually judge whether a plant is pinchable by observing its growing habits. Asparagus fern does not need pinching, because there are no small buds to scoop out from the center of the new growth.

When you pinch, you scoop out, pluck, or terminate in any way you can, the newest bud at the tip of the stem. This means squeezing the bud between two fingers and scooping it out from the center of the newest leaves. If you look at the tip growth of most plants, you will see a bud or two tiny leaves that have already burst forth from a bud. This bud is growing from the center of the top two leaves (see diagram). If you have any nails at all, it will be an easier operation than if you use your fingertips. Do not pinch the leaves too long after they have split from the bud. Ideally, you

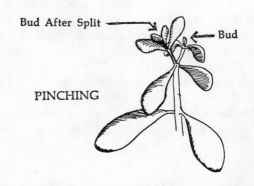

Bud After Split

Bud

PINCHING

66

should only pinch the bud, since once the leaf gets too big, pinching it will cause distortion in the shape of the next generation of leaves. I have only found this to happen to jade plants and coleus. If this occurs, don't worry. The leaves will right themselves again in the following generation. The worst that may happen to the leaf is that there will be a hole in the middle of it or that the tip will be missing.

After you have pinched there will be a rest period for the growth at the tips, and you will notice a resurgence of growth where the stem was becoming bare. Small buds will open, there may be offshoots from the main stem, and tiny offshoots that were making little progress will speed up their growth. You can either keep pinching if your plant is really straggly or watch double growth occur at the tips. I've been pinching a Swedish ivy every time I see new growth at the tips. I have been preventing any new growth at the tips so that the empty and weak stems near the soil will have a chance to fill out. All the energy is forced back to the older part of the stem. The results are very rewarding. It's like getting a whole new plant. Your plants will not only look thicker and fuller but will be stronger. They will have a bouncier, more fleshy quality in their leaves and stems—assuming that you are watering them correctly, of course. Pinch away . . . it's great for your plants. Follow the diagram, and you can't miss.

CUTTING BACK

Cutting back your plants is a form of pruning, as is pinching. If your plant has not been pinched consistently and has become long and leggy, the time has come to cut back. Plants are cut back for the same reason they are pinched. You want to cultivate stronger, bushier plants. Everyone is familiar with avocado trees that resemble umbrellas because all the growth is on top and the stem is naked. Other plants this happens to very easily are coleus, zebra plants, geraniums, wandering Jews, and aluminum plants. If you haven't been pinching out the youngest tip growth, chances are that your plants will get that long, leggy look. The same people who complain of thinned out plants are the ones who think it's cruel to cut back what seems to be a healthy plant. It is assumed that if a plant has new growth, there is no reason to cut that part away. It is very difficult for a beginning gardener to accept the fact that he is encouraging growth by cutting back a straggly stem. The longer it gets without new growth below, the weaker it becomes. There is a great deal of dormant life waiting to be awakened if it has the right stimulus. Cutting back the new growth at the tip forces the energy down to where there is nothing but stem. It is up to you to provide this extra push to insure plants a more balanced growth pattern and a healthier, longer life.

A plant can thin out close to the soil and still have healthy growth at its tips. If the plant is a fast-growing one like coleus, geranium, wandering Jew, or Swedish ivy, it is natural for the lower leaves to fall off as the new growth bursts forth. If you have been a diligent pincher, this can usually be prevented from becoming an extreme situation. If the plant has been allowed to dry out for a while, the lower leaves shrivel and fall off. If you have overwatered a plant, the leaves turn yellow and go limp, causing them to drop off. Any

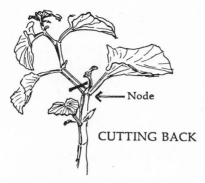

—— Node

CUTTING BACK

way it happens, you are left with very sad-looking plants.

Once you have decided to cut back, be brave. There is nothing to be afraid of. You will not ruin the plant. You can only improve its situation. If your plant looks pathetic enough, you will probably reach this conclusion yourself. Use a sharp razor blade or very sharp knife. Make sure the surface of the instrument is clean. Make a diagonal cut to expose as much surface as possible right above the leaf node (see diagram). New growth springs forth from the leaf nodes, so make sure to leave at least one node when you cut the branch all the way back toward the soil. You can judge from the bareness of the stem just how much you should cut back. Sometimes the more you cut, the better. This will give your plant a fresh start. It will give you a chance to pinch it to prevent another disaster. Place the stem cuttings in a glass of water or in vermiculite to root. (see "Stem Cutting" in chapter 7). When the roots have formed, replant the stems in the soil of the plant they were cut from. This will add a bushiness and fullness to the empty area near the soil. To illustrate why I have such faith in this method, here is a cutting-back story.

I inherited a wax begonia from someone who thought it was a lost cause. The bottom part of the stems was hard bark. There was a little new growth, amazingly enough, on the bark. This new growth was soft and green and had a few leaves here and there. I figured that the plant was old, because of the heavy bark, and that it had been revitalized many times. Reddish, pointed budlike protuberances dotted the stems near the leaves and near the bark. I knew these were buds. Leaves were inside waiting to unfold. I had the plant for about six months, but I wasn't sure whether I should pinch or not. The plant grew to be about two feet tall, varying in size according to the different branches. Leaves were dropping occasionally, but it was growing on top. Soon it started looking skinny and bare, but there was always fresh growth at the tips. Those red buds scattered all over the plant never budged.

I finally pinched the buds at the tips of the green growth in a last-ditch effort to slow down the growth. I was hoping this would force some of the energy downward to fill in the lower area. I succeeded in slowing the growth, but leaves kept dropping and no buds opened. I hated to cut it back, because it seemed like a healthy, growing plant on top, even if it was long and leggy. But, since the situation was not improving, I had nothing to lose. I cut the longest, leggiest branch all the way back to the bark, leaving one node. The rest I cut back almost as much. Within a few days, those red buds had begun to unfold, bearing new leaves to fill out the bottom of the plant. All the energy that the plant had been using to grow upward was now used to stimulate the growth of the dormant buds. As soon as this happened, I was sold on the idea of cutting back. Now I cut back everything that needs it without fear of stunting the plant forever. On the contrary, when I cut back, I can't wait to see the results.

Further corroboration appeared in the spring when I cut back my geranium. It had only a few leaves on each branch, so I cut the entire plant back. I didn't even leave a node. All that was left was a stump. It felt hard and seemed barren. If I hadn't known better, I would have thrown it out. I watered it as if it was a full plant and in a few weeks, growth was shooting out all over. New growth will emerge sooner or later from any plant you cut back. But be patient: cutting back is a trauma, from which some plants will take longer than others to recover. It will take even longer in fall and winter months.

There is another method of cutting back called root-pruning. This is done only when a plant is growing too large for a pot and you don't want to repot into a bigger container. If you take this approach, it is best to cut back the foliage at the same time. Reducing the amount of foliage on top will take the strain off the shocked roots. Checking the growth of the foliage in this way will give the cut roots a chance to heal. The energy that would be used by the growth above soil will be directed down to the shaved roots. This method is usually applied to large trees like avocados, dieffenbachias, dracaenas, and palms.

Here's how it's done: Remove the plant from the pot, making sure the soil isn't so dry that the root ball falls apart. Remove the clay drainage pieces from the bottom of the ball. Trim the roots that covered them. With a sharp knife shave over the entire surface of the root ball. Your reason for cutting is to reduce the size so that you can repot in the same pot. This will stimulate growth just like cutting back foilage above.

Keep in mind the size and shape of your pot so that you don't overcut. Just try to trim the extra stray roots not bound up in the root ball. There will be many of these, probably browned from water and rubbing against the pot. Cut off enough so that you leave an inch or two between the pot and the root ball. If you cut too much, it will take too long to grow back and you will have defeated your purpose. Now repot the plant in fresh soil in the same pot as if you were repotting

REPOTTING

One of the most important things about house gardening is to know how and when to repot your plants There are several reasons for transferring a plant from one pot to another; however, the procedure is the same for all. There are three main reasons.

First, the roots may be pot-bound. When a plant becomes pot-bound, it means that the roots have grown so dense in the soil that they have used up all the room within the confines of the pot. At this point the plant cannot get the nourishment it needs, because of overcrowding. As the foliage grows, so do the roots. It is through the roots and root hairs that plants receive their nutrients. Therefore, when the roots have no room to breathe and grow, they cannot feed the foliage. If your plant isn't growing well, it may be pot-bound. There is one way to be sure if this has happened: Remove the plant from the pot and you will see a tightly knit ball of roots. If there is very little soil in the ball and only roots, then you know it is time to repot (see diagram).

72

Potbound Plant

There is an easier and less risky method of checking for pot-bound conditions. Examine the top soil. If you see roots on the surface, you can be sure there is no room for them below. Once surface roots are visible, roots will be pushing their way out through the bottom hole. Occasionally you will see these bottom roots protruding and think the plant is pot-bound. Be careful not to be misled. Visible bottom roots alone do not necessarily mean the plant is pot-bound. To be sure, tap the plant out of the pot—then you'll know.

Second, the plant may be top-heavy. Sometimes the foliage of a plant grows at such a rapid rate that it becomes too big for the pot. This creates an imbalance, a top-heaviness that can even cause the pot to tip over. Even if the plant manages to remain upright, you may still want to repot it because it would look better. If this is the case, remember not to increase the pot size more than one or two inches (see diagram).

Finally, you may want to change pots just for the sake of changing pots. You may have gotten a new decorative pot. You may want to make a hanging plant or to combine a couple of small plants. Whatever, the reason, simply exercise caution when deciding to transplant. Repotting is a tremendous shock for all plants,

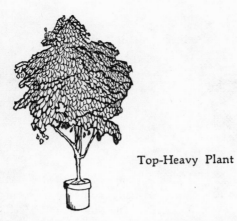

Top-Heavy Plant

so repot only plants that are healthy and strong. In fact, unless it is absolutely necessary, try to avoid doing it. If you have just bought a new plant and want to change its pot, wait several weeks before doing so, because it needs time to adjust to its new environment.

Procedure for Repotting. If you have decided that it's time for a change in pots, make sure your next pot is only a size or two larger than the one you are getting rid of. The new pot should never be more than one or two inches larger in diameter than the old pot. If you place a plant into too large a pot all the plant's energy will be directed toward strengthening the roots rather than to the growth of the foilage. The roots will be so busy trying to fill up a large amount of soil in a large pot that the leaves of the plant will suffer by not receiving their share of energy. Your plant will stagnate or grow at a much slower rate if the pot is not in proportion to the size of the plant and the amount of root growth. Repotting a plant into too large a pot can be fatal for it. When in doubt, choose the smaller one.

If you are using an old pot for the transplant, make sure it is cleaned out thoroughly. This will rid the pot of any harmful germs or insects.

Sacrifice an old clay pot and break it into many small pieces of clay. These pieces, or shards, come in handy to place in the bottom of the new pot to insure proper drainage so that the roots don't rot.

Place a small piece of broken clay over the hole at the bottom of the pot. If your pot has no hole, use four or five extra shards to create additional drainage space (see diagram).

Shard Covering
Drainage Hole

Shards Creating
Drainage Space

Now pour in a layer of charcoal bits, about ½ to 1 inch deep. Charcoal acts as a sterilizing agent and helps protect the plant against disease. It also establishes an excellent drainage process. Pots without bottom holes require more charcoal, as much 1½ inches, depending on the pot size.

Prepare your potting soil as directed in "Soil" (see below). Put it into the pot about halfway up.

Now it is time to remove the plant from its old pot. Usually it will come out easily if you turn the pot upside down and, with your hands, tap the sides and bottom of the pot. It works best when the soil is quite dry. Be sure to hold on to the plant so that it doesn't

Removing Plant
from Pot

come crashing out of the pot and break its stems (see diagram). If you have no luck this way, try sliding a dull knife along the sides inside the pot in the same way you might remove a cake from a pan. This will surely work, but be careful not to damage the roots by over-zealous use of the knife. Usually the plant will come out in the mold of the old pot. Brush away excess soil with your hand, but be careful not to disturb the roots. If the roots are wound tightly together you may want to separate them in order to give the inner ones more space to absorb the energy of the soil. This is

Loosening Plant
from Pot

done by putting a pencil into the outer roots and gently pulling it down through the ball so as to remove the tangles. Always start this process at the outer edge of the ball and work inward. If you poked the point into the center of the roots, they would surely be damaged. This is a rather tricky process and should be attempted only by the more confident gardener.

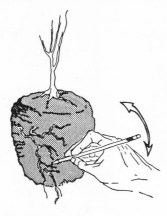

Separating
Root Ball
with Pencil

Place the plant into the new pot. Your goal is to place it between the small amount you have already put in and the amount you will put in afterward on top of the plant and around the sides to fill in the area of the larger pot. You may find that it is best to lightly press down the first layer of soil, then place your plant on the packed soil, fill in the sides, and cover the top of the plant. Keep packing the soil down so that it is firm but not too tight. It is up to you to keep experimenting with the pot, the plant, and the soil until the old plant is below the rim of the pot. It may be that halfway up is too high for the first layer of soil. After you have packed your first layer of soil and placed the plant inside the pot, on top of the soil, you will be able to tell if it's too high or too low. If the plant sits too high in the pot, remove some of the bottom soil, repack it, and try again. If the plant is too low, you can add more soil on either the bottom or top layers.

After you have covered the plant with soil and filled in the edges, check to see that there is about an inch left between the soil and the rim of the pot. This will make it easier to water.

Now take the plant in its new pot and put it in the sink under lukewarm water. Go easy on the water pressure since the soil is not settled and will overflow easily. Soak the plant until the bubbling stops and let all the excess water drain out the bottom. This is facilitated by the piece of clay you put in at the start. Let the plant dry out. See how long it takes until it needs water again. It will probably be a few days. Do not give in to temptations to water it again until it is dry. It will use up what it has and then you may give it more. Remember, you can only overwater by watering too often. You can never water too much at one time.

After you have repotted a plant, it may go into shock. The symptoms occur almost immediately if they are going to. The leaves will lose their turgidity and go limp. It may keel over completely. Don't panic or throw it out. Keep it in the shade for a few days and treat it gently. Observe it often. Treat it like a normal plant. Otherwise, you will find yourself and the plant caught up in a self-fulfilling prophecy: once a plant fails, you tend to treat it as a failure. So because you haven't given it the same care you give healthy plants, it will die. Water it when it needs it, and spray it, too. Sometimes it takes as long as a week for it to revive itself. Other times it may be just a few days. Don't give up. The plant may look dead to you, but it won't be. If you continue to care for it, your plant will come back. Be patient.

Plant in Shock

POTS

There are many types of pots on the market to choose from; the traditional red clay pot, various colors of plastic pots, decorative pots, and styrofoam. The kind of pot your plant is in helps to determine the way you care for it. Your watering procedure will be particularly affected by the pot's material.

Clay Pots. Clay pots are plentiful and cheap. Their sizes range from 2 to 10 inches and above, increasing by ½-inch steps. They are measured by the diameter of the top. All red clay pots have holes at the bottom for drainage. The best thing about clay pots is that they are porous. Thus, air entering through the clay circulates in the soil enabling the plant to breathe. Moisture and excess fertilizer are absorbed by the pot. The soil will dry out quicker than in less porous pots, so the plant will need water more often. If you have overfertilized a plant, the clay will act as a filter, ridding the soil of excess salts, and a scum of algae will form on the outside of the pot. When this happens, clean off the scum, because it can block the movement of air and moisture. Just remember, clay pots have to be scoured before they are used again.

Plastic Pots. There are two types of plastic pots. The thin, inexpensive kind come in the same sizes as red clay pots. The thicker, clear or brightly colored plastic ones cost from $1 to $6 and come in only three sizes. Most plastic pots have drainage holes or several drainage vents.

Plastic pots are not porous. They retain water longer, keeping the soil evenly moist. This is especially good if you have to leave your plants alone for a few days. On the other hand, there is greater danger of overwatering. Plastic pots are light and easy to clean. They don't break as easily as clay pots, but if you pick them up by the rim when full, they may crack. If a plant is top-heavy, it will fall over more easily in a light plastic pot. I suggest that you don't use clear plastic pots, because the roots will be exposed to light. This is an unnatural condition. It will divert the growth from the foliage to the roots.

Decorative Pots. Pots made of metal, steel, or copper are best used to house and disguise plant containers. Their chemical components and rust can combine with the soil to produce harmful effects. There are conflicting opinions on this subject. Some people have great success growing their plants in empty coffee cans and special metal plant holders. But this can be a risky business. The problem is not so much the metal as the chemicals used to treat the metal. Metal cans and pots are often covered with paint or an invisible coating containing materials that could damage the plant, especially when they mix with water. Because you don't know what is on these cans, it is better to play it safe. Put your plant in a clay or plastic pot and use the metal container to house the other one.

Decorative pots also include glazed or painted clay and plastic ones without holes. Many people make the mistake of thinking that glazed or painted clay pots are porous just because they are clay. This is not so. If a clay pot is painted or glazed on the inside or outside, the clay is *not* porous. These decorative pots do not usually have drainage holes, so it is necessary to use extra clay pieces and charcoal in the repotting procedure. Clay and plastic pots of this nature are very popular as hanging-plant containers. They are attractive and effective. However, extreme care must be taken in watering the plants because the pot will hold moisture in the bottom, making it difficult for you to know if the soil is really dry.

I bought a bright red, heavy plastic pot. It looked

beautiful even though it didn't have a drainage hole. I thought it would be clever to place a coleus already potted in red clay right into the plastic pot. The red pot was just a pretty disguise for the old clay one. The coleus seemed to be growing well, until one day I decided it looked too droopy. I removed the plastic pot just to check out the situation. To my displeasure about eight inches of brown stringy, hairy roots were hanging out of the bottom hole and draped around the outside of the pot. These roots had rotted and could no longer feed the plant. I cut off these ugly growths and re-potted the plant immediately. I concluded that when I watered the plant, the water soaked through the soil, passed out the hole, and just stagnated in the plastic pot. The water had no means of evaporating, so it collected for some time causing it to smell rancid. The roots grew down toward the stagnating water and rotted. Fortunately I was lucky, for my coleus regained its strength and is growing happily in a new red-clay pot. I put dried flowers in the fancy plastic one.

Do not let this discourage you from ever using a decorative pot, just be aware of the hazards. Most plants that die from overwatering are housed in decorative pots.

Styrofoam Pots. Styrofoam pots provide an inexpensive way for plant stores to house their produce. I have found that for some strange reason, while plants don't die in styrofoam, they don't grow in it either. You might as well use something else, since almost anything is better. The worst thing about these pots is their light weight. Just a tiny jolt will tip them over and bring the plant crashing down. I suggest you repot your plant one or two weeks after you have brought it home in a styrofoam pot.

SOIL

Obtaining the proper soil for your plants is often described as a complicated procedure. One can easily feel intimidated by fancy formulas and visions of a chemistry laboratory. It is essential to have your plants in good soil, and this can be accomplished without much trouble.

Soil has several valuable purposes other than just supporting a plant in its pot. Soil stores water, nutrients, and oxygen for the plant. Potted plants require a special soil mixture because they are confined to a small amount of soil. The roots of outdoor plants don't need such a concentrated soil because they have a larger area in which to grow and receive their nutrients.

There is absolutely no reason for you to mix your own soil from scratch. The packaged houseplant soils sold at variety stores, florists, and garden-supply shops are more than adequate. These packaged soils are mixed by professionals in large quantities. The mixture is sterilized so that there is no chance of insects disturbing it. You can buy this soil in 2-50 pound bags. Store them in a cool place, making sure to reseal the bag after it's been opened.

The "general-purpose" potting soil currently available is made up primarily of humus, an organic material of decomposed vegetable and animal matter. Although the general-purpose soil is rich in nutrients and minerals, it does have its drawbacks. It has a very fine, powdery texture. Since the soil is so fine, it tends to pack down into airtight wads when watered. Air cannot then circulate within the pot. Thus, the roots will eventually suffocate and die. Roots need a coarser material on which to anchor than the powdery packaged soil.

You can use the general-purpose soil quite satisfactorily for young plants. However, for mature plants it is better to add a few materials to the soil so that it can absorb more air and water. This is a simple procedure, requiring no fancy laboratory techniques. A little extra effort will make your plants much healthier and happier.

Packaged soil does not absorb moisture very well. It packs down too tightly causing the water to run right through it. Therefore, your potting mix needs roughage to make it springy and absorbent. In a greenhouse or garden, compost piles, made up of decayed leaves and other vegetable matter, are available. Since you won't have a compost heap in your house, you must find a substitute to mix with the soil to provide the necessary roughage. Peat moss and sphagnum moss are inexpensive replacements for compost. Either one will give your mix the required bulk because both are fibrous materials. They are also good water absorbents. Peat moss (more than sphagnum), when mixed with soil, tends to activate growth through the plant's tiny root hairs.

Another important addition to packaged soil is sharp sand. Do *not* use seashore sand: it is too soft. Quarry sand, the same sand you'd buy in a garden store, contains hard particles, which let the soil form air pockets around it. Surplus water drains out easily through these air spaces, so the soil doesn't become waterlogged. If you cannot find sharp sand, perlite or vermiculite are excellent substitutes. You can use them interchangeably, as they both provide good drainage and roughage and will hold their firmness when wet. A good soil mix should never be without sand or vermiculite.

There are many precise formulas for adding peat moss and sand to packaged soils. I have never found it necessary to measure the quantities exactly. To repot a plant into a 6″ × 6″ pot, just put some packaged soil into a bowl or cardboard box. Estimate how much soil you will need to fill the pot three-quarters full. Add a handful of peat moss and a handful of sand. Mix it thoroughly. You will then be ready to proceed with repotting. If you need a lot more soil, try to combine the ingredients in the same proportions.

These are merely guidelines to follow when making your soil mix. When you become more experienced, you will be able to adjust your mix to what works best for your plants. Just remember that all soil mixes need a combination of water-holding and water-draining materials, so make sure you strike a reasonable balance between potting soil; sphagnum or peat moss; and sand or vermiculite. Take your pick. *Don't* be afraid to experiment.

FEEDING

The process of feeding and fertilizing plants is an often discussed and disputed one. I have always asked myself, "What, when, and how should I feed my plants?" Admittedly, I have never felt very comfortable with the whole idea of plant fertilization, because somewhere in my mind I think so-called miracle-grows are a fake and are used only by cheaters. I always thought my plants were doing fine without any chemical assistance, but plant people were always talking about what kind of food they used. I began to feel that anyone dedicated to happy, gorgeous plants just has to help them along with plant food. I was left with no choice; I had to get some and try it. After a lot of experimentation with various plant foods and methods of feeding, I have decided plant foods can in fact be quite beneficial for certain types of plants.

Plants get their nourishment from two sources: Through the foliage, they breathe in gases (primarily carbon dioxide) from the air; and through the roots, they absorb soluble minerals from the earth. There isn't much we can do about the air, but by using plant foods we can help the soil replenish itself. Normally, nature takes care of this job with shifting topsoil, decaying vegetable matter, and natural fertilizers. Soil is composed of many ingredients, the most important ones for healthy growth being nitrogen, phosphoric acid, and potash. Commercial plant foods contain these same ingredients but in different proportions. Producers of plant food are required by law to state the formula of their product on the outside of the container. So, you will see something like "7-6-19" printed under the name of the product. This means:

Nitrogen	7%
Phosphoric acid	6%
Potash	19%

The numbers representing the percentage of each mineral are always placed in the same order.

If you object to chemical additives, you can always use organic animal manure as a fertilizing agent. It will work just as well as the commercial product. However, manure has a rather unpleasant odor and is very difficult to store conveniently in your home. Plant foods are odorless, and a small box will last a very long time.

When you decide it's time to buy plant food, maybe

because your plants are droopy and lazy, you will be faced with about 25 different types on the store shelf. How do you know which one to buy?

First, you will notice several different brand names. Hyponex, Ortho-Grow, Miracle-Grow, to name a few. Then you will see that there are three or four different formulas put out by each company. I have found that the general-purpose plant food seems to be the best and the safest. If you're not sure about how much nitrogen one type of plant needs, you can be sure that the general-purpose food will be adequate. The other type you may want to buy is the special formula for the African violet. Many people find this plant very enjoyable, and when successful, it will bloom flowers throughout the year. If you have African violets, I recommend that its special plant food be used only according to the directions on the label.

Another complication you may run into is that plant foods come in different mediums. There are liquids and powders that go directly on the soil. The only type that is safe and worthwhile is the powder that is diluted with water. The liquid can be dangerous because you often tend to feel you haven't fed the plant enough. The liquid tempts you to figure that "just a little more can't hurt." That little bit may *kill* the plant. You have to be extremely careful with plant foods because they are very strong and can easily burn the roots of the plant. The two major causes of dead droopy plants at home are overwatering and over-feeding.

I bought some plants during the summer at a nursery in the country. The plants were quite inexpensive compared to city prices, so I was pleased at finding such a bargain. At the checkout counter, the woman was giving away free packages of a powdered plant food. I took it, anxiously hoping that it would liven up some of my older, sadder plants. I discovered that it was one of those "just sprinkle it on the soil" types. I knew that this wasn't the procedure I had previously followed, but I decided to follow the instructions exactly. Even if the plants died, my scientific experiments with plant foods would be carried one step further. The directions said to sprinkle a teaspoonful on the soil every two weeks. I did this operation for about two months, trying to determine if there was any change in the plant, a maranta. The powder remained white or gray as it lay on top of the soil, doing nothing for the plant's good looks. The powder never seemed to penetrate the soil, even though I kept the plant on its regular watering schedule. As the weeks went by, the powder began to darken, so that at least it blended with the color of the soil. Meanwhile, the plants were not getting any healthier and I was beginning to get discouraged about the experiment. Finally, one day the maranta just keeled over and died. I had no idea what could have happened until I realized the food powder had been building up on the top soil and had eventually penetrated to the roots. There was so much powder, it had probably burned the roots immediately, causing the plant to die. After that episode, I discontinued using any fertilizers because I was so frightened of their potency.

Now I will use only a powder diluted in a large quantity of water. Even these solutions can be harmful to the plants if they are not administered with great care and patience. Remember, plant foods are not "miracle grows." They will only replenish the soil with the nutrients needed for healthy growing plants.

It should be emphasized again that plant foods are very strong and must be used with extreme care. You will find it helpful if you try to feed your plants on a regular basis. The schedule will depend on your specific plant. I would recommend no more than once every two months. In this way you can be quite sure that you won't be overfeeding the plants and thereby risk burning the roots. Follow the directions exactly on the plant food box. The directions usually call for a teaspoonful diluted in two quarts of water. If you do not have a two-quart container, measure how much your container will hold with a measuring cup and adjust the amount of plant food accordingly. Then put the correct amount in the empty container and add about a cup of very hot water. This insures that the food will dissolve completely. Then add the rest of the water to complete the solution. When you have made sure that the chemicals are all dissolved, go ahead and water all your plants in the same way that you always do. Feeding your plants will replace that day's watering; it is not given in addition to the regular watering.

This feeding procedure should help your plants to stay strong and fresh—as long as you don't overdo it. If a white scum develops on the outside of the pot, this is the signal that you have overfed your plant. There are a few other indicators of overfeeding. There may be new growth, but it will be very weak and the plant may wilt. A white crusty scum may develop on the soil's surface as well as on the outside of the pot. This crust is a buildup of excess salts caused by too much fertilizer. When this occurs, stop feeding for a few months. Scrape off the scum, and water thoroughly to wash the salts through the soil.

There is another feeding method that is very unusual

yet effective. A solution of equal parts water and ammonia can be used regularly. When I first heard this I thought it sounded absolutely ridiculous. The idea of feeding plants my strongest, most unpleasant-smelling household cleaner seemed like a dangerous way to strengthen plants. I discovered that ammonia is composed primarily of nitrates. Plants need a good deal of nitrogen in the soil, so using ammonia is not as ridiculous as I had imagined. However, there is one problem with this method of feeding, and that is that plants need other minerals too, like potash and phosphoric acid. Your plants will not get a balanced diet if you feed them only ammonia. It will probably be best if you stick to the general-purpose plant food, knowing the plants will get just what they need.

PESTS

The subjects of pests and diseases are unpleasant. No one wants their plants to be harmed by bugs and ugly fungi. Just as in the case of your own health, who wants to know to what diseases they are susceptible or even what their symptoms are? Unfortunately, however, these invasions of good health exist whether you like them or not. And so it is important to be aware that houseplants, like all growing things, are not immune to pests and diseases.

I don't want to give the impression that you have to be a plant hypochondriac to have happy, healthy plants, but you should be able to recognize that your plant's unhealthy condition could be symptomatic of an infestation of some kind. It is consoling to know that less than 10 percent of houseplant deaths are caused by bugs or disease. The remainder are caused by improper care—an excess, or lack of, water, fertilizer, sunlight, humidity, heat, and so on. Thus, when you notice an unhealthy or unusual condition in your plant, first make sure that you are giving the plant what it needs to grow well; if you are, then you may find that the plant is really sick.

You may be saying to yourself that the whole idea of getting plant pests in a city home is ridiculous. How can such animals live in your clean house? Well, they can. It is difficult to know how pests actually get into your house, whether they come in the window or they breed there. More likely, they are brought in on new plants. Most plant shops receive their stock in large quantities from nurseries in Florida and the tropics. Unfortunately, many shopkeepers never spray their newly arrived plants. The pests survive the long journey and make themselves at home on your houseplants. If you bring a plant home from the country it may have some bugs on it. You may buy fresh flowers that have bugs on them. All of these are possible causes of plant pests. To avoid a severe infestation, check the plants or flowers carefully before you bring them home. If you suspect some unwanted bugs on the plant, isolate it from the other plants so that the problem doesn't spread. When you are sure that the plant is healthy again, you can take it out of isolation.

There is one sure way of avoiding a pest attack on your plants: by practicing prevention on a regular basis. In the same way that people try to protect themselves against colds and other illnesses, you can try to insure that your plants stay healthy and sanitary. I have found that spraying my plants with a weak solution of Ivory Liquid twice weekly helps keep pests to a minimum. This soapy solution cannot harm the leaves or stems, it can only keep them clean and somewhat immune to pests and fungi. Some people like to spray their plants every month with a plant insecticide as an added precaution. This is all right, although such chemicals are not really helpful to the plants and can interrupt their growing process. I have an aversion to chemical sprays, especially when used indoors, and so, I resort to them only if severe infestation persists.

It is often difficult to know if your plant has bugs on it, because most of the common pests are so tiny you wouldn't normally see them. Therefore, the only way you can tell is if you notice the plant has an abnormal appearance. The leaves may be mottled with brown or white spots. The stem may appear to have brown nodes on it. White stringy deposits may build up in the area where leaves meet stems. These are symptoms of some types of pest. They are not symptoms of poor care, as are browning leaf tips, loss of leaves, or yellowing leaves.

Generally, I have found that the same method of treatment works for everything, no matter what the pest. The specific variations are listed below under each type of pest. When you suspect that there is a pest on a plant, isolate it immediately from the other plants. If you can see the bug, pick it off the plant. (Make sure to wash your hands thoroughly after this operation so as not to contaminate any other plant.) Turn the pot sideways, holding the soil so that it doesn't fall out. Wash the plant in soapy water (dishwashing liquid) until all traces of the pest are removed. If it is a plant too big to move, spray it heavily with the soapy solution. Rinse the plant, using a wet sponge, with plain lukewarm water to get the soap off. This procedure should remove the infestation; however, it may not get rid of all the eggs. It will be necessary to repeat the whole process every few days until the plant returns to good health. When the plant starts growing again and all the symptoms are gone, you can put the plant back with its friends.

A word of advice about chemical pesticides is necessary. Use them with extreme caution. I try to avoid pesticides wherever possible, because I don't trust them. Even though the chemical will surely rid your plant of pests, I have never been sure how much damage it can do to the plant. Malathion is the most common pesticide for indoor plants. It comes in a plain spray bottle and an aerosol bomb. Never use the aerosol bomb, because too much chemical evaporates in the air and is left there for you and the other plants to breathe. The spray bottle, however, is controllable; the pesticide goes where you spray it. Diazianon is another chemical, recommended especially for its residual effect. It is a very strong pesticide commonly used for garden pests. Be very careful with it, and follow the directions on the label exactly. In general, try the nonchemical approach before you resort to the chemical method. You will breathe easier.

Mealy Bugs. If you see white cottony balls along stems or on the underside of leaves, you know that mealy bugs are moving in. These bugs suck the sap from plants, eventually killing them. Their sticky secretions make shiny patches on the leaves. To eliminate mealy bugs, dab each white bug with a Q-Tip dipped in rubbing alcohol or witch hazel. The bugs will shrivel and fall off. Be careful to touch only the bug and not the plant (or as little of it as possible).

Wash the plant thoroughly as described above. Because each mealy bug can lay up to 600 almost invisible eggs, the alcohol treatment must be repeated every few days until all the bugs and eggs are dead. Just wiping off the stem and leaves with plain water won't help. Before you blink an eye, the bugs will have reappeared.

Red Spider Mites. These mites are generally red, although some are green. It doesn't really matter what color they are, because they are microscopic in size. The only way to tell if you have them is by noticing fine white webs woven in crevices, in joints, and on leaf undersides. Foliage becomes speckled with yellow or brown spots.

Usually both webs and mites can be washed away with a strong spray of soapy water, followed by plain water. In very severe cases, spray with Malathion according to the manufacturer's directions. Don't ever use Malathion on jade plants, ferns, or kalanchoes.

Scales. Scales look like rounded brown shells congregating on the underside of leaves and along the stems and main veins. They remind me of shiny turtle-like warts. Since scales cannot move, they stay in one spot until you discover them and remove them with your fingernail or a strong stream of water.

Do not confuse scales with the spore cases common to ferns. Fern spores are lined up in a symmetrical pattern, whereas scales are more haphazardly placed and found on stems as well as on leaf undersides. Malathion can be used in very bad infestations, but carefully, and in a well-ventilated area.

Aphids. Aphids are small insects found sucking on new buds and leaf undersides. They can be gray, red, yellow, brown, green, or black. Aphids cause foliage

94

to yellow and die. They also deposit a shiny, gooey substance (honeydew) that attracts sooty black mold to the leaves. To treat for aphids, pick off any visible insects and then follow the general washing instructions. If necessary, use Malathion or nicotine sulphate.

White Flies. These pests are the most harmful to your plants because they can fly from one plant to another. For this reason also, they are very difficult to exterminate. White flies are tiny sucking insects that cause leaves to yellow and die. You may notice them when you touch a plant and little white things flutter about. Like aphids, they secrete honeydew. White flies lay eggs on the underside of leaves. The transparent green larvae stick to the plant, drinking its sap and doing it terrible damage.

If you catch the flies early, washing with soapy water will probably kill them. However, if the problem persists, spray with Malathion or just throw out the plant.

Cyclamen Mite. This mite makes itself at home on African violets, begonias, ivy, and geraniums. Leaves and flowers become stunted and distorted. Leaf edges curl up, giving the leaves a cup shape. Cyclamen causes such horrible damage that the best thing to do is dispose of the plant altogether. Sterilize the pot before using it again.

Soil Pests. Use of a packaged sterilized potting soil greatly reduces the chances of having pests in the soil. There are no outward signs on the plant that tell you there are insects in the soil. The only way to find them is by actually seeing them moving around in the soil.

Repot the plant right away. If you use the same

pot, clean it thoroughly and use all new soil. You will not be able to remove all the soil around the roots without murdering the plant. When the plant is in new soil you can get rid of the leftover pests with a nicotine solution. If you can't repot the plant right away, this remedy will work wonders. Soak an ounce of tobacco (pipe tobacco is cheap) in a bowl of water. Let it sit for an hour or so until the water is dark brown and very smelly. Pour the liquid through a strainer into the soil. The nicotine will kill the bugs immediately but will not harm the roots of the plant.

Cockroaches. Some homes are plagued with cockroaches. Occasionally, roaches will be seen around the pots and soil of your plants. Roaches need water and moisture to live. If they cannot find it anywhere else in your house, they may go to the plants because the soil contains a lot of moisture. They will not get in the soil. In fact they don't really harm your plants, although roaches have been known to eat very young plants. Harmful or not, no one wants roaches on their plants. Do not use your ordinary roach spray, because it is toxic to plants. Malathion will work, but Diazianon is better because it has a residual effect. That means that it will work to kill the roaches for several weeks after you have used it.

A Few Words of Caution. Don't use insecticides designed for control of household insects. They don't work for plants and are often harmful to them.

When using insecticide sprays, ventilate the area well and spray only those plants that are infested.

Do not use insecticides in aerosol bombs.

Careful and sanitary care of your plants will prevent pests from ever becoming a problem.

6 NINETEEN OTHER PLANTS

ASPARAGUS FERN
(Asparagus sprengeri)

Asparagus Fern

The so-called asparagus fern is in fact not a fern. Its foliage is light and airy, creating the lacy effect of ferns. It reproduces by seed, while the fern reproduces by spores. There are two species, but they look almost exactly alike. The *Asparagus sprengeri* has a coarser, lighter green foliage than the *Asparagus plumosus*. The lighter and smaller *plumosus* is a climber. It will creep all over like a vine if given guidance. The *sprengeri* is bushier and has long, graceful branches up to four feet long. Both look perfect in hanging pots, especially in bright or sunny windows.

Their foliage is Kelly green and takes the form of needlelike projections. The feathery quality of the branches is displayed especially well when allowed to cascade. If cared for correctly, the *sprengeri* will become lush and robust. But watch out for its tendency to yellow a great deal, especially when it is sending up new growth. Just cut off all the yellow branches so that they don't drain energy from the rest of the healthy plant. I am convinced there will always be a certain amount of yellowing taking place on the asparagus fern. Don't worry about it unless the plant is totally thinned out, in which case you are doing something very wrong. Asparagus ferns really flourish in lots of sun but bright light all day will suffice. They also must have a very moist or humid environment. I know one that is sprayed *every day*, whenever its owner gets the urge. It is also watered *every day*, a little bit, to keep the soil constantly moist. This asparagus fern is going berserk. New growth is shooting up all over the plant—up from the soil and branching from the stems.

It is important to become acquainted with the foliage in the different stages of its life cycle. New stems rise from the soil without the needlelike leaves. The stems are long, skinny and bare, except for a small cluster compressed at the tip. As the name implies, it looks just like an asparagus. Only after the stem is about a foot long does it begin to fill in. If you are not observant, you might assume this bare new stem was really an old one that had lost its leaves. When I first got mine, I made this mistake and cut back about six new shoots.

If the plant becomes unwieldy, it's fine to cut it back to shape it. Cut anywhere on this plant, and it will add strength to the entire plant. Otherwise, let it hang long and low, taking pleasure in its abundant quality. Division is the easiest and most successful method of propagation. These are plants that can easily be divided into two or more small plants, depending on the sizes and fullness of the original. As the plant ages, it may develop small, white, scented flowers, but don't expect them: it depends on the maturity of the plant. One last word—watch out for the thorns on the stems. They can really hurt.

FERN

Ferns (except staghorns) always evoke images for me of Victorian conservatories filled with these lush plants in wicker baskets or in hanging pots. Rooms filled with Oriental rugs, Tiffany fixtures, and multicolored talking parrots to complete the scene. Ferns were very popular at the beginning of the twentieth century and succeeded then because of the lack of dry central heating. These days, the first thing to be

Maidenhair Fern

Boston Fern

considered when contemplating a fern for your home is whether your environment is sufficiently humid to allow the fern a long and happy life. All ferns sold as houseplants are the ones grown in tropical rain forests. Usually only terrariums or greenhouses can offer the right conditions of temperature, humidity, and light.

Although the fern is delicate, lovely, and just the thing you want in your house, consider that of all the houseplants mentioned as growable, the fern has the most do's and don'ts attached to it. Plant manuals are filled with descriptions of the fussiness of the fern.

They give advice like "Water the fern a great deal but don't overwater it," or "The fern likes shady places but can perish from too little light." After reading these warnings you still won't know how to care for a fern and will assume the life of a fern is so tenuous that you'd rather not chance it. But, be brave. With a little knowledge, some love, and a lot of luck, maybe you *can* raise a healthy fern.

The most common varieties are Boston ferns, sword ferns (*Nephrolepis*), and hybrids of both. These are the simplest to care for and definitely the hardiest. Boston ferns have the thickest and largest fronds. The rest display gradations in delicacy, laciness, and size. Another popular variety is the maidenhair fern (*Adiantum*). It is much more fragile and difficult to maintain. The soil should be kept constantly wet. They enjoy less light than the other ferns.

No matter which one you buy, it will need more moist air around it than any other plant in your collection. The usual methods recommended for this are pebbles in the tray below the pot to provide constant water evaporation. They also enjoy a warm misting a few times a week. In addition, add lots of peat moss to the soil to insure the circulation of air within the soil. Some say daily watering is essential, while others say the soil should dry out completely before watering again. Whichever way you do it, everyone agrees that the base of the pot must not sit in water. The roots of a fern rot more easily than those of any other plant, so be sure to rest the pot on top of pebbles or gravel to prevent the pot soil from becoming waterlogged. At this point, it is worth mentioning that fern roots are very easy to burn with fertilizer, so don't use it if you can help it.

I had a very lovely hybrid fern and lost it. To this day I am not sure what I did wrong and have rationalized that a conglomeration of factors led to its demise. That fern was doomed from the beginning. I didn't water it daily, for fear I would overwater it. Then the leaves turned brown and brittle giving the impression it was too dry. When I began to water it more often, it still made no difference. I sprayed the foliage with warm mist everyday, trying in vain to compensate for a dry apartment created by the steam heat. By this time, the fronds were browning worse than ever. Now everything pointed to too much water. I was getting frustrated and impatient with the fern. This impatience was transmitted to the plant, and didn't help its response to me. I didn't perservere with my fern, and sure enough, it died.

If you haven't been scared off by now, here are a few hints that might prove useful. The fern likes warmth without dryness. Don't put it in the sun, because it will burn the fronds very quickly, leaving them brown and brittle. Cutting off the browned parts will only cause further bruising and browning. The fern frond is so fragile that anything other than gentle touching will cause damage. Don't crowd your ferns with other plants. Let it hang free or stand alone, so as not to cause bruising.

The fern enjoys filtered light and can even sit in the shade for periods of time, but it is difficult to say just what "too much shade" really is. From all I've heard, ferns grow well under artificial light, so that's worth a try for confirmed fern-lovers.

Ferns reproduce themselves by spores. The brownish dots lined up symmetrically on the frond underside are spore cases. Don't think your fern is covered with some disease or pest when you catch a glimpse of these spore cases. You can propagate ferns in the home by division. Good luck with ferns—you may need it!

STAGHORN FERN
(Platycerium)

Staghorn Fern

There are strong conflicting opinions on the viability of maintaining a thriving staghorn fern indoors on slabs of bark, on which they are now being sold by expensive plant shops. In tropical conditions this fern has evolved to the point where its lower leaf attaches itself to a moist mossy area high up on a tree. The plant derives its name from its hornlike fronds. Like all other ferns, it needs plenty of water, diligent misting, and some light but not direct sunlight. If you choose to hang your staghorn fern on the wall because you bought it on a slab, don't hang it in sunlight. Take it down to water it about twice a week; others say daily. Dunk it in the bathtub in lukewarm water for about 15 minutes to make sure it is thoroughly soaked. It is no use watering it while it's on the wall. It will never receive enough water and will eventually perish. There are some experts who say it will die anyway if kept indoors in this manner, but others say staghorns will grow well in pots in a soil mixture with lots of fibrous material like peat moss and sand. The staghorn fern doesn't like heavily packed soil. You could also try lining a wire basket with sphagnum moss and fill it lightly with peat moss, sand, and soil and hang the basket in a warm spot. Then there are others who say you'll never raise a staghorn fern successfully except in greenhouse conditions. Pay your money and take your chances.

JADE PLANT
(Crassula)

Jades are succulents. They are also aptly called Chinese rubber plants because of the Oriental appearance of their leaf configuration and arrangment. Most jades are deep green and have smooth, fleshy oval leaves. As the plant matures, the lower stem becomes brown and barklike giving the impression of a full-fledged tree.

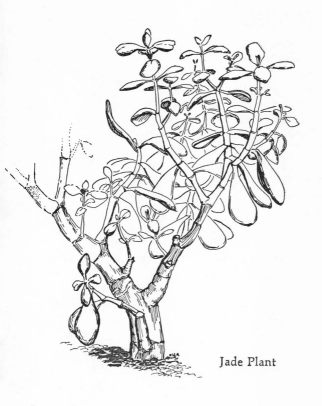

Jade Plant

Jades are indigenous to hot, dry desert regions
Instead of having regular foliage, they have evolved
thick, bulbous leaves and stems that store water to
guard against dry spells. If you break a jade leaf-disk
in half, you will see its inner network filled with water.
The waxy coating of the leaves and stem helps contain
the water supply. It also protects the plant from too
great exposure to the sun. This is why watering your

jade is the most important part of its care. It is best to let it dry out completely to a sandy textured soil before watering again. Supposedly, this plant can go for a substantial period of time without watering—a consolation for the forgetful. But, the experience I have had with my jade contradicts this. My jade dries out usually within three days, at which point I give it a hefty watering. When I first bought it, all advice pointed to giving it as little water as possible. Within a week's time, the jade was losing leaves all over and other leaves were getting wrinkled and limp. Something was wrong: a healthy jade leaf should have firm, glossy leaves like hard, thick rubber to the touch. Once I started watering it more frequently, it flourished. The only lesson I can draw from this is that, as with all plants, you are the one to decide what your plant needs.

The average jade grown indoors grows to about a foot, but as the years go by it can grow up to three or four feet. I know a jade-lover who has at least a dozen large jade trees basking in direct sunlight all day as if in their native habitat. They give her fragrant white blossoms and lend a touch of the Orient to her decor. She tells me though that the less sun they receive, the less of a possibility there is of flowering. Besides, her trees are about 15 years old. The tree itself also becomes more thickly clustered, fuller in shape and less elongated, the more sun it gets. If it isn't receiving enough sun it will stretch toward the light and lose many leaves. Even consistent pinching will not help a jade that isn't getting its share of sun.

When transplanting a jade, which only has to be done once a year or even less, remember to be very careful with the roots. If they are overly bruised, the plant can be seriously affected. Instead of following the usual repotting procedure, let the plant stand a few days after repotting and then give it a light watering. Jades can be propagated from leaf or stem cuttings. It is almost impossible for it not to root because of the water stored inside. So, although the plant has a delicate root system, it doesn't take incredible expertise to root it. If you are interested in increasing your plant collection, put stems, rather than leaf cuttings, in sand or vermiculite, since stems are hardier and will grow faster.

ROSARY VINE
(Ceropegia)

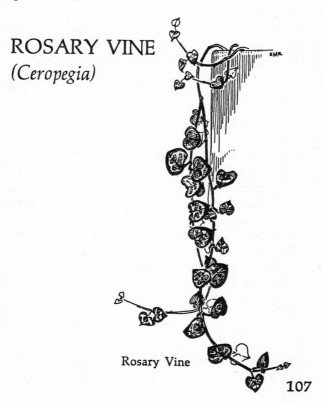

Rosary Vine

This succulent is an extraordinarily delicate-looking plant, but its appearance belies its basic hardiness. It is an unusually strong hanging plant. The tiny leaves are almost heart-shaped and spaced far apart on the stem, which can give it a stringy look if you aren't careful. It will grow well without sun but needs about as much light as is provided by a northern exposure. The vines can grow as long as six feet but should be pinched often to avoid weakness and thinning. The tiny blue-green or gray-green leaves are spotted and range from the size of your thumbnail to the size of a quarter. This plant can't take too much water. It can actually survive for weeks in dryness, but overwatering will kill it very quickly. One good way to keep it looking full and healthy is to place a vine on top of the soil and pin it down with straight pins or hairpins to root the stems in moist soil. This can be done at the top of the plant or in a new pot. I have mentioned this form of propagation in relation to nephthytis, philodendron, devil's ivy, and other vinelike plants. Make sure to stick the pins right through the stem, preferably at the point where the leaves grow from the node, to promote root growth. You can also propagate it by cutting off a vine and planting it without rooting it in water. Put half under the soil and let the other half hang down. If you're lucky, tiny flowers may blossom at the end of the summer. Remember to keep it in a warm place out of drafts but don't worry about humidity: it can bear very dry environments.

IVY

There are three basic groups of ivy sold for indoor use. Grape ivy (*Cissus*) grows with little light and erratic

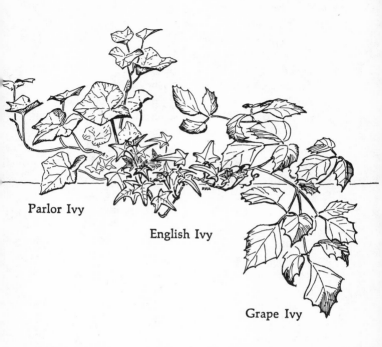

Parlor Ivy

English Ivy

Grape Ivy

watering as an attractive hanging vine; it can be easily trained to grow upward with a string or garden stick. The leaves are delicately carved triangles, with sharp points at the edges. Its compound leaf has three metallic-green leaflets growing from one stem, adding to the bushiness, which can easily be retained by pinching and cutting back. The stems have tiny tendrils that curl around almost anything for support. This gives the grape ivy a mind of its own. It will tolerate warm and dry apartments as long as it is sprayed a few times a week. Let it dry out before rewatering. This ivy is a "can't miss."

Then there's the English ivy (*Hedera*). This is another story completely. English ivy comes in many different varieties. Some are heart-shaped, round, ruffled, star-shaped, or curled. Some have completely green leaves, while others combine green with yellow, white, or light green. They range from leaves the size of a thumbnail to ones four inches long. They cascade or can be trained upward. Unfortunately, English ivy grows best outside but is sold as an "easy" houseplant by florists. I have had many pots of English ivy that looked beautiful when I bought them but within a month turned yellow and lost most of their leaves. English ivies are happy in cold temperatures indoors. English ivies are also very prone to the red spider mite. If they are grown in pots in a cool window, you may have success.

A friend of mine lost a green English ivy and got so angry at it that she left it out on her window sill. Between rain and her splashes of water, the ivy came back in a couple of months. She had totally cut it back, and when leaves started to grow, she decided she liked it again and brought it inside. She keeps it in the open window, as it loves the cold air. She keeps the soil moist and has used the pinning and winding method to make it fuller on top and to propagate easily. This is another good reason to keep the soil moist. Pinch off stems at tips to increase bushiness and cut back often, rooting those stems in water. Ivy will live in water and give off roots, as do philodendron and devil's ivy. Leave it in water or plant it in soil according to your whim.

Parlor ivy (*Senecio*) is the third basic type of ivy sold for indoor use. It is larger and less delicate than the others but a little hardier in that it withstands heat. It too is a vine. Its multilobed leaves are larger than those of the other ivies, growing up to five inches long. They are a darker, almost blackish, green and stick straight up from the vine on a longer stem than the other ivies. Parlor ivy is treated in the same way as English ivy and grows really well in plain water.

AFRICAN VIOLETS
(Saintpaulia)

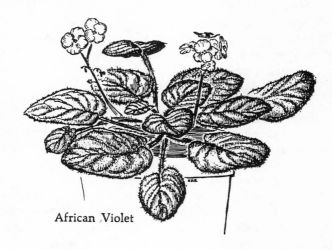

African Violet

African violets are advertised as one of the most popular and easy-to-grow houseplants around. These little flowering plants originate in Africa but are not violets at all. The name comes from the color of their flowers, which can be pink, blue, or white as well as violet.

Contrary to popular opinion, African violets are not so easy to grow. They require a lot of care and attention, especially if you want them to flower year round, as they should. The biggest problem with African violets is that everyone recommends a different approach to their successful care. I have never had much success with them, so I am hesitant to pass on "definitive" instructions, as do most plant books and plant people. But here are a few general pointers.

African violets seem to do best in bright, indirect light. Only in mid-winter, from November to February, should they be in direct sunlight. You will have to determine the best place for your African violets. If the leaves become bleached and blotched, they are getting too much light. If your plants are flowering poorly and getting elongated leaves, they are not getting enough light. Many African violet growers use artificial light with great success. Either fluorescent or incandescent bulbs placed about 12 inches away for 14 hours daily seem to give the best results.

African violets are very temperamental about the air they live in. Coming from the African jungles, they like very humid air that is not too hot or drafty. If the air is too hot or dry, buds and flowers will fall off. If it's too cold, they will grow very slowly and the leaves will curl down around the edges. To increase the humidity, keep the plants on a tray of pebbles with water in it. It is a good idea not to spray African violets, for this causes white spotting on the leaves.

The most important factor in proper watering of these tender plants is warm water. African violets can be watered from above or below the pot to keep the soil just slightly moist. Do not let them dry out. They probably will not need water every day, but check the soil just to make sure. And remember, use only warm water.

Patience and tenderness are the keys to healthy African violets.

ZEBRA PLANT
(*Aphelandra*)

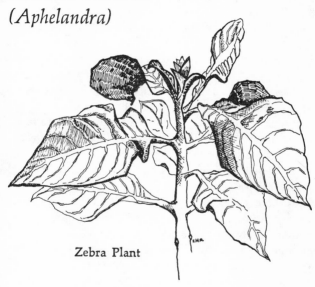

Zebra Plant

Beware of seduction by the exotic zebra plant. This plant is practically impossible to raise for any long period of time in the home. I was warned by an expert horticulturalist to resist the temptation to buy one, even though they were very beautiful and unusual. Zebras become very long and leggy within a few months, leaving only a few leaves on top and a bare stem below. Even with consistent pinching, it is hard to control the drop-off rate of the leaves. The reason for this is that most homes cannot provide the hot, humid atmosphere this South American jungle plant craves. So keep in mind this plant may only last for a few months, depending on its environment and a little luck.

Like the maranta, the zebra has uniquely lavish markings on its leaves. When you buy them in plant shops, they usually have one branch filled with six-inch leaves. The rich grassy green of the leaf has a creamy white vein system. These veins provide not only stark coloring but indentations for tactile delight. Besides these wonderful curvaceous leaves, there is a bonus of a large, sunny, yellow flower nestled in the center, looking regal on a throne of green foliage. This plant is really hard to pass up. I couldn't.

Within a few weeks of my purchase, I noticed the luscious yellow flower was shrinking with increasing speed. The spikelike flower is made up of many cruciform florets with trumpetlike pistils. As the plant grows, the new green leaves form at the base of the flower. The top leaves of the flower die and get picked off one by one. Soon, the entire yellow flower disappears, giving way to two stems growing independently. A gaping hole is left in the center where the flower used to reside. When I first got my plant, it was my impression that the flower was turning into green leaves—a magic trick of the first order. I didn't understand what was really going on until the resident horticulturalist at the New York Horticultural Society told me that it was a physical impossibility and dismissed the whole idea as pure nonsense.

In all cases, the flower will disappear and the plant

will take on the look of a small tree. The stems are dark brown and very smooth, like wax. They appear barklike but feel almost like plastic or hard rubber. If you pinch the plant consistently to force the growth upward from the base, you might get a new stem up from the soil or a new shoot off one of the main stems. Spray the leaves a great deal with warm water to keep the air moist. Ocassionally, place a plastic bag over it and seal it with wire to simulate greenhouse conditions. Try gravel or pebbles in the tray below too.

The zebra plant loves water. It took me a while to realize that I didn't have to wait for the soil to dry out before the plant needed more water. The leaves simply went limp and lifeless, signaling that it was thirsty. Within an hour of watering, the leaves were perked up and standing at attention. Even those thick stems flop over completely and hang over the side of the pot if left without water for more than a few days. But when water is supplied, the stems regain their turgidity in a few hours. The best way to propagate a zebra is by air-layering. So, go ahead and buy a zebra plant. Do whatever you can to make it last long and even fluorish. Maybe you will be the one to find the key to making this plant thrive outside a terrarium or greenhouse.

PIGGYBACK PLANT
(Tolmiea)

This is a hairy-leaved, delicate plant. The stems and leaves are covered with a light fuzz, giving piggy-

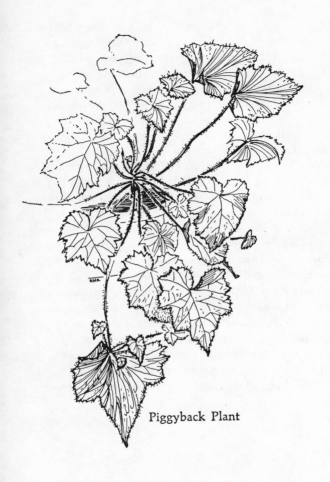

Piggyback Plant

backs an unusual texture. The leaves grow up to about 15 inches, but many come smaller than that. The piggyback plant takes its name from the manner in which it reproduces. Each long-stemmed leaf produces a miniature version of itself at the point where the leaf is attached to the stem. The leaves seem to grow in clusters, one on top of another.

A word of caution if you have bought this plant or are contemplating purchasing one. They are often sold in small pots as seedlings but usually in hanging pots or large pots offering you, at first glance, a bushy, healthy, luscious plant. More than many other plants, the piggyback will not stay this way without proper care, and even then, it is temperamental and has strange habits. The mistake most people make is in the watering. This plant must have moist soil at all times. This does not mean overloading with water everyday. It does mean checking the soil often to see if it is drying out. It must be kept damp at all times or else the leaves will shrivel up and die. These leaves dry out and become brittle very quickly if they aren't getting enough water. Remember there's a difference between watering a plant when the soil is still wet and watering it when there is a slight dampness. If the soil crumbles when you finger it and isn't soggy or muddy, then its time to water again. Most people I know who have had a piggypack plant did not water it enough, causing the entire plant to dry up and die. But, they held on to the pot and watered it regularly as if there were still foliage and in about eight weeks the plant came back much healthier and grew happily. It likes any kind of light as long as it is moist and is in a humid environment. So, don't give up if yours looks as if there's no hope. Either wait for it to return or cut back the sick part, to add energy for new and healthy growth. Once you've got the hang of piggybacks, they're really easy. Propagate by leaf cuttings.

COLEUS

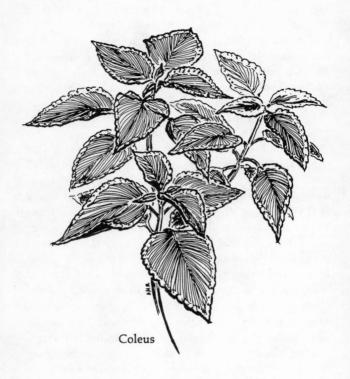

Coleus

The coleus is multicolored and fast-growing. The leaves are 1–4 inches long, and the plant can be as high as 2½ feet. It is immensely hardy and will grow right back, no matter where it is cut off. Even if it falls and breaks a main stem, it will come back stronger than before. With a minimum of care, coleus will flourish for even the most inexperienced gardener.

118

The coleus comes in a wide variety of colors and combinations. Magenta, purple, and maroon are the most common colors. These are usually mixed with yellow and green. Their color gets brighter the more they are exposed to sun, but this isn't necessary to grow them. Filtered light is plenty for a healthy and gaily colored plant. The coleus is incredibly phototropic, which means that it grows toward the light. In order to insure a balanced plant, it is necessary to turn them every day or so. It's a real treat to turn a coleus at the end of each day and be faced with a burst of blazing color for the evening.

The coleus needs a good deal of water. Since it uses up water very quickly, you can let it dry out almost completely before soaking it again. Coleus, unlike most other plants, will go limp as soon as it needs water. Watch for this signal, but don't worry when it happens—it is practically impossible to overwater a coleus. Spray it with plain water about twice a week. Spray it with Ivory Liquid solution once a month to protect it from mealy bugs, a common enemy.

The most important way to keep a coleus looking bushy and thickly foliated is to pinch it often. This prevents it from becoming leggy and top-heavy. The more often you pinch, the better the plant will look. If you are not diligent about pinching, the bottom leaves will yellow, die, and fall off. The plant will lose the lush quality you loved about it to begin with. (See "Pinching" in chapter 5.)

The coleus is propagated quickly and easily by stem cuttings. You may find that the coloration of a newly planted cutting becomes washed out and even colorless; this is not unusual. The color will return with a few additional inches of new growth.

GERANIUM
(Pelargonium)

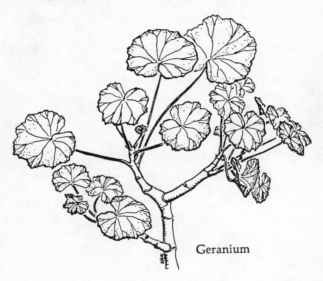

Geranium

Even if you are not familiar with plants, you certainly know and can recognize geraniums. They are often seen brightening up window boxes and planters outside cafes or neat country homes. Their cheery red, pink, or white blossoms always add gaiety, color, and a pleasant smell to a plant collection.

Like African violets, geraniums require more care and attention than most people think. If you want them to be full-blooming houseplants the year round, you must have good direct sunlight. Geraniums need at least a few hours of sunlight everyday; thus, a southern exposure yields the strongest plants. During the hot summer months, however, geraniums should not be exposed to sun all day long, because they can dry out too much. If your plants are not getting enough light, flowering will be reduced and growth will be irregular.

Unlike most other houseplants, geraniums are not tropical plants. They do not like hot or humid air. Because geraniums grow best in a dry atmosphere, they are well suited to home cultivation and should not be sprayed with water. Spraying causes brown spots on the leaves and will ruin the flowers if water lands on the buds. Geraniums must be well ventilated. They will be happiest in day temperatures of 60-70 degrees and 15 degrees lower during the night. If you keep your geraniums on a windowsill, away from radiators, the cold window glass or air-leakage should provide the necessary coolness.

Geraniums are not particular about the soil in which they live. A general-purpose mixture (see "Soil" in chapter 5) will be fine. Oddly enough however, they like to be tightly potted. The lower leaves on one of my geraniums started to yellow very rapidly. I thought the plant was probably pot-bound. It was, but I made the mistake of repotting it into a much larger pot, to save myself the trouble of doing it again later. I found that the leaves grew very well but that it hardly flowered at all. So, if you have to repot, only use the next-largest size pot and pack down the soil very tightly. Your chances of having full-flowering plants will increase considerably.

When it comes to watering geraniums, everyone has a different story. Some say, let the soil dry out, while others say, keep it moist. It is very difficult to decide which is best. Geranium stems have excellent water-retaining properties. Therefore, the leaves do not wilt when the plant needs water. The only signal you may get from your geranium is a sudden yellowing and loss of bottom leaves. When this occurs, your plant desperately needs water. Always water them from the top, and don't let water sit in the dish below.

The most common problem with home-grown geraniums is their gawkishness and lack of flowers. These unattractive qualities can be remedied by constant and thorough pinching. Geraniums usually start a strong growing period in the spring. Before this period begins, you should pinch all leaf and flower buds before they open. This will be a rather frustrating time for the plant, since no new growth is allowed to develop to maturity. However, a strong root system will thrive, helping the plant to grow many long-lasting flowers. You will have to check the plant every day for new buds because they will come very quickly once they start. You may be reluctant to pinch new buds, especially flower buds. Don't be. Pinching now will mean bushy, healthy plants later. It is worth it, particularly if you have scented geraniums. When they are pinched or cut back, they fill your house with a luscious smell. You will think you are in the country, surrounded by dozens of multicolored geraniums. Have a nice trip.

RUBBER PLANT AND FIG TREE
(Ficus)

Rubber plants and fig trees are relatives, members of the genus *Ficus*. Both plants will potentially grow to

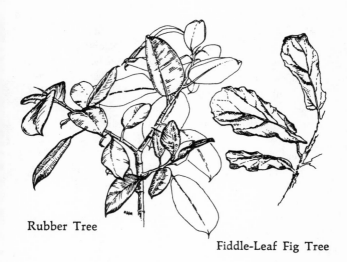

Rubber Tree

Fiddle-Leaf Fig Tree

be large trees. This can easily be done in your home environment, under poor light conditions. They can be purchased at a plant shop for more reasonable prices than most foliage houseplants. Their sizes cover a wide range: small ones come in eight-inch pots, and huge multibranched trees, in tubs. The leaves on both grow anywhere from 6 to over 12 inches; the broad oval leaves are thick and heavy and deep glossy green. Some, being hybrids, have shinier, waxier coatings than others. All the ficus sold in the United States are hybrids, so their characteristics will be seen to vary slightly.

The most important thing to remember in caring for ficus trees is not to overwater them. The soil should remain barely moist at all times. Try to avoid

123

letting it dry out completely before watering again. Your best bet is to water it only twice a week. This naturally depends upon how dry your house is. Check the soil with your fingers to find out, because there are no hard and fast rules. The only trouble with ficus is that too little or too much water makes the leaves turn yellow and fall off. Once this starts happening, the tree will go downhill very rapidly unless you remedy the watering situation. If the soil turns over and is only slightly moist to the touch, you know it is time to water.

Keep these trees in a cool location out of direct sunlight. Ficus plants do well for long periods of time in dark areas of the house, but unless they get some light, they will die. They grow best in bright, filtered light. Any supplementary artificial light will do also. The new leaves grow up from the center of the stem in a red pointed bud. If you desire a bushier, multi-branched tree, you have to start pinching to force the growth down and outward. Don't worry if a white sticky, gumlike substance gushes forth when you pinch or cut back. It will soon dry and harden, and new shoots will spring from the points below the cut.

The main difference, therefore, between a rubber plant and a fig tree is what they look like and what they produce. The fig tree has leaves more irregularly shaped. They are wrinkled and brittle. The entire vein system is white or cream-colored, making a distinct pattern on the leaf. Don't expect figs, if you are growing this as an indoor plant. The rubber plant is often multibranched, with large, very smooth—sometimes waxy—leaves. Usually only the main vein down the center of the leaf is distinctly creamy white. About 150 years ago India or Burmese rubber trees were the source of rubber for the world. Now India rubber trees are used as houseplants. Brazil and Africa are now the main producers of rubber.

The only other care Ficus would appreciate is a sponging once in a while to rid the large leaf surface of soot and dust. Ficus can be propagated by air-layering.

SWEDISH IVY
(Plectranthus)

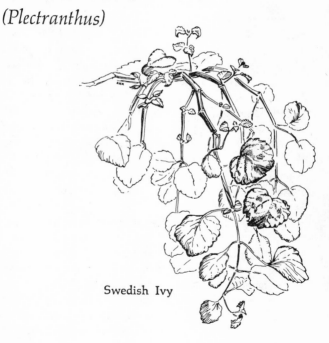

Swedish Ivy

Once the technique of watering a Swedish ivy is mastered you can grow long, swooping pots of it. The Swedish ivy, which is neither Swedish nor a true ivy, is almost a succulent in its drinking habits. The leaves are substantial and waxy, although flexible and shiny, unlike most succulents. My experience with Swedish ivy is probably typical of those who have trouble growing what are supposed to be easy plants to care for. Because of its minor succulent quality, it retains a certain amount of water in its leaves. Therefore, even if the soil is *almost* dry and you are tempted to water it, don't do it! Wait until the soil is *completely* dry before thoroughly soaking it. I lost two gigantic Swedish ivy plants in hanging pots by overwatering them. Whenever the soil was almost dry, but not sandy, I would feel compelled to water. Normally, I wouldn't have watered them, but the leaves seemed slightly limp and the beautiful shine of the leaves was gone. I automatically assumed that it was thirsty. After all, when leaves go limp, the first thing I think is that they need more water. Soon the ivy started turning yellow on all the larger, more mature leaves. Many of these yellow leaves were dotted with blotches of brown. Having lost two plants by simply ignoring the signs and giving more watering, I reversed the process on my third Swedish ivy.

At first, the same thing happened. I bought the plant during the summer in Massachusetts. It stayed alone in the house up to four days without anybody to water it. It never received direct sun, only filtered light. You can be sure that after four or five days, the leaves were slightly limp, but otherwise the plant thrived. It grew to almost three times its original size in three months, looking graceful and delicate. The vines hung lower and lower every week. All the branches grew toward the light, so I turned it often for the sake of balance. When the summer was over, I brought this incredible specimen, purchased for $3, back to New York. I was sure it would be traumatized by the air and the smaller amount of light it was going to get. I was overanxious, and that brought on a recurrence of the overwatering syndrome. Everytime the leaves lost their initial glow after watering, I got like a mother hen. Out came the watering can, before the soil had dried to a sandy consistency. Within a few weeks the yellowing and browning started, and then I knew for sure what the problem was. I let the soil dry out totally, all the while aching to water it because the leaves were limp and dull. It took about seven days for the soil to become sandy. Then, I took the most luxurious pleasure in giving that plant the soaking of its life. It began perking up almost immediately, and by the next day, it's summertime loveliness had been restored.

Naturally, I had plucked all the yellowed leaves off the plant and pinched the tip of every stem to insure new growth on top. This should be done a great deal to achieve a bushier growth. Even while the soil was drying out, I continued to spray the leaves, to increase moisture in the area around the foliage. Swedish ivy likes to be sprayed and will reward you with the most refreshing, intoxicating fragrance. The odor is unlike any you have ever encountered. On the other hand, the flower, which blossoms in the spring or fall, is not particularly enchanting. If you want it, then keep it. Otherwise, simply pinch it away when it appears. This will direct the energy toward foliage growth rather than toward the flower.

The Swedish ivy leaf comes in a variety of shapes. The larger ones have scalloped edges. Some have shinier surfaces and are a richer green. Basically, they all need the same treatment. A bright, filtered light is ideal and in my opinion better than sunlight which tends to drain its color. Some people find sunlight a real boon to this plant. You will have to test this out on your own, assuming that you have a choice of window exposures.

The shinier, scalloped variety is the hardiest for propagation purposes, but all Swedish ivy is a cinch to root. If rooted properly, you should be able to get a birthday present together of a hardy Swedish ivy in a small pot for a friend if you plan ahead about one month. Simply cut at the main stem and follow the instructions in the chapter on propagation (chapter 7). Remember, the shorter the stem cutting, the quicker it will take root. Place the cutting in a glass of water, and pinch the tip carefully. If you examine the stems of Swedish ivy, you will see roots already popping up all over. The water just hastens the process and softens them. Don't be afraid to cut a few of the vines for rooting or cutting-back purposes. It will only serve to revitalize the entire plant. In this way, you not only gain a new pot of Swedish ivy but enhance the beauty of the original plant. Don't forget—less water means more pleasure.

CROTON
(Codiaeum)

The slightest draft will cause a croton to start shedding its leaves, go into shock, fade in color, and never recover. I may be overstating my case, but I have found crotons to be very difficult plants to raise under any but junglelike or greenhouse conditions. I saw my first croton on Tobago, an island that can only be described as a paradise on earth. It is the place where the model for Robinson Crusoe had his adventures. The flora of this island is extraordinary in its variety. Nestled among the coconut trees and banana trees are fabulous multicolored crotons. They are about three feet high and very bushy. Each leaf is about a foot long and coarse in texture. The leaves are oversized ovals that look as if someone had splashed paint all over them.

Croton

Sometimes the leaves are bright red with green, orange, and yellow or combinations thereof. When young, the leaves are mostly green, but their colors become more pronounced as they mature.

Keep the croton in a warm sunny window if possible. It needs a great deal of bright light, if not direct sunlight. This will not only keep it from becoming leggy but will also enrich its colors. The croton loves water and, like many other plants, will droop when it needs more. Your best bet is to keep the soil moist at all times and to place the pot on top of a bed of pebbles, to create constant humidity around the foliage. Spray the leaves at least once a week, if not more often, to give added moisture and to guard against mealy bugs and red spider mites, the croton's common enemies.

Sometime you might be lucky and come across crotons that are even more gaily colored than the common one. Don't be surprised if they come in yellow, gold, pink, purple, and white. One leaf may have five or six colors. Some leaves may be scalloped, while others are broad and lobed. Whatever they look like, crotons can be propagated by stem cuttings or air-layering.

BEGONIA

There are so many different kinds of begonias you may never find out what you've got. But it doesn't really matter, since they all require basically the same care. If you can identify the type of begonia you've got from the three major groups, then you are well on

130

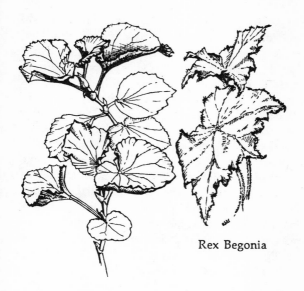

Rex Begonia

Wax Begonia

your way to knowing what is necessary for your plant. There are over a thousand species and hundreds of varieties of begonias. For identification purposes you only need be aware of three groups: tuberous-rooted, foliage, and semperflorens.

Tuberous-rooted begonias are noted for their large, luscious, extravagant flowers. They are usually grown out of doors in garden beds or window boxes, so most likely you don't have one of these unless you have a garden outdoors too. They are more difficult to raise than the other two groups and are not considered houseplants.

Foliage begonias are a more common household begonia and come in the rex, spotted, metallic-leaf, and beefsteak varieties. They are known for their extraordinary leaves with many varieties in color, pattern, and texture. They come in purples with metallic spotting; reds with greenish luminous blotching; or silver with green, red, or purple markings. Many of them have a fuzziness or hairiness on the leaves and stems that combines with the coloring to look truly bizarre and weird. Some are even scary-looking, evoking the feeling of Venus's-flytraps in horror movies that unfold a leaf and swallow the heroine. Foliage begonia won't gobble you up, but if you are into unusual-looking plants, this is the variety for you. Foliage begonias need less light than the flowering begonia. Filtered light or partial shade is fine. If they are placed in sunlight with their leaves wet, they will burn. If your foliage begonias are brown at the edges or brittle, they are probably getting too much sun and not enough water. Don't spray them with water as you do other plants. They don't like wet leaves. The foliage types are easily propagated by leaf cuttings. Place the leaf in a rooting medium and cut some of the main veins. This makes it easier for roots to form. Hold the leaf down flat on the medium with pebbles or a pin.

Finally, there is the most popular of the begonias, the semperflorens or wax begonia. This produces flowers continually (*semper florens* means "always flowering") in pink, crimson, and white. They make good plants not only for the house but for window boxes. The foliage varies from tiny bronze leaves to large greenish leaves with bronze edging. Some of the larger wax begonias are green on top, with a smattering of silver or white that looks as if someone had dripped paint on the leaf. The underside is reddish brown, and the edges are scalloped. If your wax begonias aren't blooming now, have patience; eventually, they will, with proper light and temperature. They need cool temperatures and good light, but too much sun will burn the edges of the leaves and cause browning and shriveling. Let water touch the leaves as little as possible.

Contrary to popular opinion, begonias are sensitive plants and require the right balance of humidity and light. Some advise keeping the soil damp, while others suggest letting the soil dry out completely before soaking again. I would agree with the latter, since in my experience, dampness wilts begonias.

Constant pinching and frequent cutting back are *essential.* I cannot emphasize this strongly enough. If you aren't diligent in this, the leaves will drop off below, as with most plants. You will be left with long empty stems and all the new growth at the tip. Of all the plants, the begonia makes the fastest comeback of all. The new buds on a wax begonia are such positive reinforcement for your pinching and cutting efforts that you won't be able to stop once you start.

Begonias often grow really well for a long period of time and then get sick for no apparent reason. Either it's lack of light or you haven't pinched and cut back enough, thus weakening the plant tremendously. Also, once begonias become diseased there is no saving them. This may be too dogmatic of me, so if your begonia gets sick, give it a chance.

A most important rule for begonias is to pot them lightly. When mixing your soil, make sure you add extra sand or vermiculite and extra peat moss. This will guard against tightly packed soil. Charcoal in the soil will bring out the leaf color and flower hue. Begonias grow best when their roots are crowded, so don't repot them very often. Only repot if the root ball has totally filled the pot.

Propagation of begonias is simple and almost guaranteed. Make stem cuttings of semperflorens about four inches long, and put them in water for about a week. Then, when rooted, you can add them to the original pot or start a new one. Leaf cuttings of this variety yield very weak plants, so stick with stems. You can root the cuttings in vermiculite if you want. Either way, you should not have much trouble with the semperflorens.

FITTONIA

Fittonia

134

The fittonia have fabulously patterned leaves that really knock your eye out when you first see them. Their nerve network is so intricate that the dark green leaf looks almost quilted. The two varieties are silver-nerved fittonia and red-nerved fittonia. These plants really only do well for extended periods of time under terrarium or greenhouse conditions. But, with a little extra help, it may do very well in your home. Keep the soil moist at all times. To keep the moisture enclosed, place the pot on top of pebbles lining either a tray or, even better, another, larger pot. Keep some water mixed in with the pebbles to create constant evaporation. These extrahumid conditions are absolutely essential for the life of a fittonia. There is no other way it will live. Light is not important, since they, being jungle creepers, are accustomed to the shade of the jungle floors. Light will not harm them, but hot, direct sunlight will dry them out and burn their leaves. These creepers are easy to propagate by stem cuttings. Start new plants often because after about a year, they will become long and straggly outside the terrarium. Spray them often—they'll need it. If the leaves start to drop off, it means the air is too cold for them, so move them to a warmer location. Pinch them often to keep them from getting straggly.

WANDERING JEW
(Tradescantia and Zebrina)

There are two basic kinds of wandering Jews; the *Tradescantia* and *Zebrina*. Both genera consist of long

Wandering Jew

trailing vines that grow quickly and look best in hanging pots. The zebrina has a gaily colored green and white leaf that always reminds me of wintergreen or peppermint candy. Its leaves range from two to six inches in length. The vines are strong and will grow indefinitely with proper care. The tradescantia has a greater variety of color, usually green tinged with silver on top and a rich burgundy on its underside. It grows the same way as a zebrina.

I had a tradescantia for about eight months hanging in the window. It cascaded gently downward and then reached up toward the light. When I took cuttings from this plant to start new ones for myself and friends, I noticed a new quality about their growth. They are very phototropic. Whichever way you prefer to grow them, they will stretch toward the light source. I placed a small pot of new cutting below the window level and the vines grew straight up to the light.

The most important thing to watch out for with a wandering Jew, especially the tradescantia, is the thinning out process that takes place at the top of the plant near the soil. This is natural because of its rapid growth rate. The mature leaves near the soil dry up and die. This leaves a scrawny and empty stem above, while there is healthy growth at the tips. If you want to keep this plant looking full and healthy, you must continually pinch it to suppress tip growth, encourage branching, and stimulate dormant life. Also, take stem cuttings, root them, and replant them on top again. This recycling procedure is essential for maintaining a healthy wandering Jew. It will not take care of itself. Don't be afraid to cut back: it has a tremendous regenerative capacity. Usually a new shoot will erupt from the point where you have cut. This serves to create the fullness you seek.

It is comforting to know that you simply can't fail at rooting a stem cutting from a wandering Jew. Within a few days after you have placed one in water, hardy white roots will appear at the nodes. It is then that the stem should be planted immediately. If the roots get too long, they weaken. Don't worry about the stems that don't take once they have been planted.

They may go into shock after planting but should revive after a week. If they don't, then don't waste your time with them. Throw them out and start some new cuttings.

Wandering Jews like light or sun. The more light the plant is provided, the richer its purple tones. There is another vinelike plant called the purple heart, which looks like a fatter, hardier version of the wandering Jew It grows in much the same way but has less leaf-loss. It also demands diligent pinching and propagates very easily.

CALADIUM

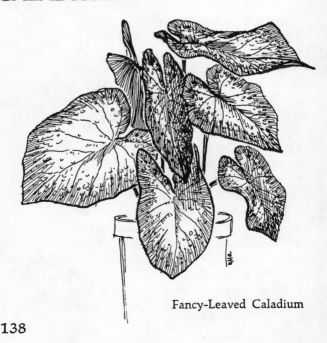

Fancy-Leaved Caladium

Fancy-leaved caladiums are only part-time foliage plants because for several months out of the year they shrivel down to the soil and look as if they are dead. This happens during their dormant period. Their leaves are huge, broad arrowheads, like nepthytis but much wider. But their coloration is more like coleus. The color range includes white and shades of pink, red, and green. Their texture is like parchment, and they have very pronounced vein configurations. They cannot have full foliage in both summer and winter. So, if your caladium was bought when it was doing beautifully, in winter, by summer it will be gone and should be stored in a warm, dry place and given no water. Don't throw it out. It has dormant buds and will come back fully by the next season. It likes to be warm in its growth period and takes either full sunlight or filtered light. Spraying with water will keep it fresh longer. When the leaves start dying, it means the dormant period has arrived, so stop giving it as much water and repot it when its growth period starts up again. Propagate caladiums at intervals so that you have at least one healthy one at all times. Division is the best way to propagate them.

For beautifully colored leaves . . . coleus is the better buy.

NORFOLK ISLAND PINE
(Araucaria)

Christmas trees are more expensive every year, so here's an inexpensive answer to your wildest dreams:

Norfolk Island Pine

a real Christmas tree all year round. The Norfolk pine is an evergreen that is symmetrically tiered just like any pine tree. Watch out for its needles: they're fragile and don't enjoy being handled much. Although it's a conifer, it doesn't like the cold. So don't be fooled by its outdoorsy appearance into placing it ouside during the winter. It will lose all its foliage, and you will lose your Christmas tree.

Indoors is another story. The Norfolk pine doesn't like hot rooms either, so find it a cool place in the house, making sure its not in a draft. If the lower branches begin to drop off, it means its too warm, so move it fast before it begins to look like an umbrella. It likes bright light or even full sunshine, except in the summertime when it gets too hot. Strangely enough, Norfolk pines are hardy and survive under adverse conditions. They will do well under poor lighting but then should not be kept as moist as those receiving more light. Otherwise, keep the soil evenly moist all the time.

Mature Norfolk pines grow as high as 200 feet in their native habitats of Chile, Australia, and New Guinea. But as houseplants they have a very slow growth rate. Some may only grow 2½ inches each year, and others, as much as 3 feet. The growth potential depends upon how much food, light, and moisture it is receiving. As a matter of fact, it only needs two or three feedings a year, so go easy on the fertilizer

The method of propagation of pines has a direct effect on both the growth rate and the cost of the plant. The easiest way of growing them is from seed. This is how the ones sold for houseplants are produced. When rooted, cuttings from the whole top yield slower-growing more compact plants. Only one cutting like this can be made from the original plant because the cuttings from any other part of the tree grow lopsided and can't be sold. So, you can propagate your plant by a terminal cutting but you'll be taking a chance.

7 PROPAGATION: MAKING MORE FROM WHAT YOU'VE GOT

There are several ways to increase your plant collection without spending a lot of money on new plants. In this section, four common methods of plant propagation are discussed: cutting, division, air-layering, and winding and pinning. Use the chapters on successful houseplants to determine which method is appropriate for your plant. You will find them all quite simple and extremely rewarding.

STEM CUTTING

Stem cutting is the easiest, and often the fastest, way of propagating new plants. It can also be beneficial to the mother plant, because cutting back or pruning keeps plants full and healthy.

Be sure to take cuttings only from your healthiest plants, and do not take too many cuttings at one time, to avoid shocking the plant. If the plant becomes stunted for some time after the cutting, you have probably made too many cuts. It usually takes from two to six weeks to bring a healthy new plant into the world, so if you want to give a plant as a gift, you should plan ahead. Don't worry about the time of year: cuttings will grow almost anytime under the proper conditions. However, some plants have dormant periods during which they do not grow at all; it is then best to wait until they start to grow again. If you are doubtful, then wait until early spring or summer to be guaranteed success with any method of propagation.

One general rule to follow when making cuttings is to *always* use a razor blade or sharp knife. Never use scissors, as they squeeze the stem, causing it to rot.

Procedure for Stem Cutting.

1. Make a diagonal cut (to expose as much surface as possible) from about four to six inches from the tip of the section, just above a leaf node.
2. Pinch off the tiny bud at the tip. This forces downward growth, causing roots to grow more quickly. Pinching is especially important with Swedish ivy and coleus.
3. Cut off the leaves at the bottom of the section, again to encourage rapid rooting (see diagram).
4. Place the cutting in a glass of warm water or a container of vermiculite or perlite. If you choose the less expensive water method, make sure to put fresh warm water in the glass every few days. If you choose the vermiculite, soak it well with water and insert the cutting just deep enough for it not to come out. To speed up the rooting process, cover the cutting and container with a plastic bag. Sandwich bags or vegetable and fruit bags from the grocery store are fine because they retain moisture while allowing air

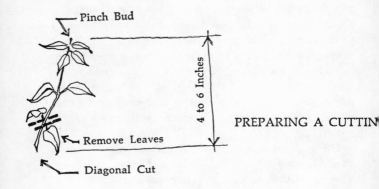

Pinch Bud

4 to 6 Inches

Remove Leaves

Diagonal Cut

to pass through. This little makeshift greenhouse gives the cutting the humidity, warmth, and moisture needed to propagate. You probably won't have to add more water to the vermiculite but you should check it occasionally to see that it remains evenly moist.

5. Put the cutting in a lighted place but never in direct sunlight.

The length of time required for cuttings to root varies for each plant, so it is essential that you keep a close watch on them. This is more difficult when using vermiculite, so be very careful when you gently remove the substance to look at the roots If you have put several cuttings from one plant in the vermiculite, just check on one of them, because, since they tend to grow at the same rate, there is no need to dig up more than one.

144

Do not let the roots get too long, because they will weaken the plant and are not worth the effort of planting. When the roots are one to two inches long the cutting must be put in soil. If you have used vermiculite as a starting mixture, then you can wait a week or so before transplanting.

Procedure for Planting.

1. Prepare a pot with shards, charcoal, and soil as described in "Repotting" (in chapter 5). The soil should fill about one-third of the pot.
2. Carefully remove the cutting from the water or vermiculite container, making sure not to damage the roots.
3. Place the cutting upright in the soil, holding it in one hand and gently putting the rest of the soil around the cutting with the other hand. Press the soil down very carefully so that it fills the pot, leaving ½ to 1 inch around the rim.
4. Soak with water in the sink until the soil stops bubbling. It probably will not need water for a few days after this procedure.
5. Keep a close watch on the new plant, treating it like a fragile child, until you feel it has become adjusted to its new home.

If you are putting a cutting into an already growing plant to make it fuller, your procedure will differ slightly: Using a pencil or pen, make a deep hole in the soil, making sure not to touch any already planted stems. Place the cutting in the hole, and fill the hole with soil. Water the plant and watch it grow fuller and healthier!

There are many plants that propagate through stem

cuttings. I have found that coleus, wandering Jew, Swedish ivy, begonia, and philodendron reproduce especially quickly and satisfactorily.

LEAF CUTTING

This method of propagation is similar to the method described above. This method is best suited to plants such as African violet, fittonia, and maranta. Make a diagonal cut where the leaf joins the stem. Put the leaf in vermiculite, cover container with a plastic bag, and within a few weeks it should have enough roots for it to be planted in regular soil. Then follow the instructions for planting listed above.

DIVISION

Division is another method of propagating new plants while thinning out overcrowded mature plants. The process is no more complicated than the other ones; however, you do have to know which plants can be divided.

Plants that send up new growth directly from the soil are divisible. In such cases, the new stems will not be attached to the mother plant above the soil, although their roots may be entangled. Ferns, asparagus fern, spathiphyllum, wandering Jew, and Swedish ivy are in this category.

Plants that develop identical offspring near the main plant or some distance away can be divided. These small offspring are called offsets. Spider plants and sansevieria will form offsets if planted in a fairly large pot. The roots of the main plant are connected to the offset by runners in the soil. Runners allow a sansevieria to develop its own root system.

These are just a few general hints to help you decide which plants you can divide. If you keep in mind that plants with single stems, bark, or cane stems cannot be divided, you should have no problem. For example, jade plants, dracaena, and succulents cannot be divided. In order to control their growth, you can cut them back or air-layer them.

Procedure for Dividing Plants.

1. Only perform division when the plant is in a healthy growing condition. If it is dormant or ill, dividing a plant will kill it, not heal it. If you're not sure, wait until spring.
2. Tap the plant out of the pot as you would in a regular repotting procedure. If the soil is somewhat moist, the roots will not be damaged in the process.
3. Shake as much soil off the roots as possible; then, with your hands, brush the rest away. As more roots are exposed, you will have to be careful not to break any roots.
4. When most of the soil has been removed from the ball, the plant may separate itself, depending on what kind of plant you are dividing. If this happens, let it.
5. Now you should have at least two separate clumps of foliage with roots. If some roots are still entangled, try to separate them as gently as possible.
6. If you can't separate the roots with your hand, use a sharp knife. The cutting process must be

done quickly and without hesitation. The roots are as anxious about the operation as you are, so you must get it over as fast as possible.

7. Do not saw away at the roots. Try to sever them in one stroke. Pretend you are using a meat cleaver to separate chicken bones.

8. Assuming the plants and your hands are still intact, the worst part of the job is completed. You can now repot each plant separately. Do this right away so that the roots aren't exposed to the air for too long.

9. Remember these are young, vulnerable plants, so take good care of them.

AIR-LAYERING

Air-layering is a method of propagation used for plants that have long main stems with either bark or cane covering. The rubber plant, dieffenbachia, and dracaena are the most common in this category. If you have one of these plants and it seems to be growing too tall and leggy, you should cut it back. Instead of just cutting off a large section of the stem, air-layering simultaneously prunes the old plant and creates a new one.

Procedure for Air-Layering.

1. Using a sharp knife, make a *vertical* cut in the stem a few inches below the lowest branch. Make the cut two inches long and approximately halfway through the stem. Roots will grow out of this opening, but the top of the plant will still be fed by the roots in the soil.

2. Cut a piece of clear plastic about 24 inches

square. (The plastic bag that soil comes in is as good, as is a dry cleaner's bag.) If you use a very thin plastic, you will probably need a larger piece.

3. Cover the stem around the area of the cut with damp sphagnum moss or peat moss.
4. Wrap the plastic around the moss, and use a string or tape to close the plastic bag tightly at the bottom.
5. From the top of the wrapping, water the moss thoroughly, and then tape it closed (see diagram).
6. Whenever you water the soil, water the moss. In about six to eight weeks you will see roots peering out of the moss where you made the incision.

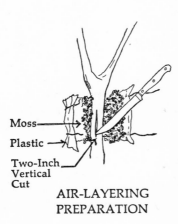

Moss

Plastic

Two-Inch
Vertical
Cut

AIR-LAYERING
PREPARATION

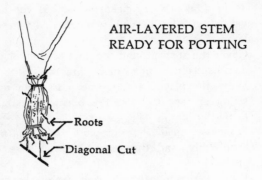

AIR-LAYERED STEM
READY FOR POTTING

Roots

Diagonal Cut

7. With a knife, cut off the stem just below the moss package. Remove the wrapping gently, and plant the new rooted stem in potting soil. Since it will be a large section of the stem, plant it at least halfway down in a large pot so that the roots have space to develop (see diagram).

Now you have a brand new plant and you will be delighted that you put up with that odd wartlike dressing for so long. If the remaining stem of the original plant is quite long, you can propagate new plants from it also. This is done by cutting the stem into 10-inch lengths. Lay each cutting horizontally, half-buried in vermiculite. Cover the dish with a plastic bag. Eventually shoots will develop from the top side of the cutting. When you see these shoots, you will know that roots have grown below. When the top shoots are 2 inches high, remove the stem from the vermiculite and cut the cane into workable sections. Include one or two top shoots in each small section, making sure not to cut through any of the roots. Each one of these rooted sections can be planted in soil so that the horizontal stem is covered by the soil and the new shoot is exposed to the light.

WINDING AND PINNING

This method of propagation is not only an easy way to increase your plant collection but another means of forcing new growth on spindly, thinned out, bare-on-top plants. The same principle is used here as with leaf cuttings or stem cuttings, which are placed in a rooting medium. What you are trying to do is force new roots to grow from stem tissue, and this is simply another way to do it. The best plants to experiment winding and pinning with are creepers or vinelike plants like pothos, nepthytis, Swedish ivy, philodendron, rosary vine, monstera, and wandering Jew. All these plants tend to lose a great deal of growth on top near the soil and look naked on the vine. This type of plant has tiny bumps or pimplelike projections at the nodes. These are dormant roots just aching to burst forth. Actually, if sprayed consistently they will grow long and stringy. If these plants were wild in nature, they would root in the ground by means of these projections. What you are doing at home is helping them to do the same thing. You are pinning them to moist soil to stimulate growth.

Cutting back and pinching solve part of the problem but when the plant is really looking bald, try this. Your philodendron has become straggly and weak. If your soil is no longer rich, add an extra layer to the

151

top to accommodate some new growth. Take the stem of the philodendron and wind it all around the top of the pot, arranging it on top of the soil. If there are a few stems to wind, leave room for all of them. As you wind, pin the stem down firmly to hold it fast to the soil. Various kinds of pins may be used, depending on how thick the stems are or how big the plant. For smaller or more delicate plants, a straight pin may suffice, in which case simply stick it right through the stem into the soil. This will break the special growth tissue inside the stem. This tissue contains cells that divide to produce new growth. Make sure this tissue (stem) is injured in some way when you are pinning, because this stimulates faster rooting. If your plant is larger and needs something heavier than a straight pin to hold it down firmly, use hairpins or bobby pins. These come in all sizes, so use any size that meets your needs. With hairpins and bobby pins you are not automatically breaking the tissue. Try to crush the stem a little while fastening it down with the pins. Fasten at a node, because this is wnere it will root the quickest. If fastened firmly enough, there is no doubt you will have crushed the stem a little.

Before you know it, the plant will look like new again. The thinner growth will be pinned to the topsoil, adding dimension and size to a tired old plant. If there is a lot of difficulty winding the stems you can cut them off and then pin them on top. If you have some stems left over or have decided to start a new plant, take the cut stems (no matter how long they are) and do the same pinning and winding process on top of a new pot of soil. Crock the bottom for drainage as you would when repotting a plant with its root system intact. Fill the pot with your soil mixture.

After you have performed the pinning and winding, water the soil well, making sure it is soaked throughout. Watch for the water to drain out the bottom. Be careful with the pinned stems, since they are still not rooted and are fragile. It is important to keep the soil moist after this process, because it will provide a more receptive medium for rooting. Your plants will become much stronger and healthier and will look infinitely better. The roots should take quickly, but be patient. If it is not spring or summer, it may take longer, since nothing grows fast in the fall or winter. Before you know it, shoots will start to grow up from nodes, and the new growth on the original stem will continue to thrive. Don't forget to keep these plants in a warm place and to spray them often to provide continual moisture.

All I can say is, don't be afraid to experiment. If you don't try, you'll never know if it could have worked. You have nothing to lose but a cutting. You will be surprised how successful you can be with a process that may sound complicated at first but is really very easy and fun to do. The first time I tried winding and pinning, I didn't trust my ability or the dependability of the process, so I used a rosary vine that was so far gone that I didn't feel that it mattered if it failed. I wrapped the skinny little runt of stem around the top of a fresh pot of soil and in just a week new growth was popping up all over. Reinforced by my success, I did it to an English ivy. What had been a scrawny specimen at first burst forth with new growth in just a few days. This is the way I keep my wandering Jew bushy on top. Once you get the hang of it, try it with whatever you want. You never know what you'll discover.

8 STARTING FROM SCRATCH

AN AVOCADO:
DON'T THROW AWAY THE PIT

Growing an avocado plant is a popular practice among urban gardeners. It is quite a simple operation, and if done properly, will result in a huge healthy tree with large dark green oval leaves. Unfortunately, many people do not care for their avocados correctly, so that the tree looks like a very tall telephone pole with four or five leaves at the top. Like many other houseplants, avocados must be cut back and pinched often so that the tree grows to be full and bushy. My avocado is one of my prize plants. I have had it for about four years; it is now 8 feet tall and 6 feet wide, with many branches coming off the main stem. Every time I look at it, I am proud that I actually started that tree from a small helpless pit.

It is difficult to know which avocado will grow best just by looking at them in the store. I've always tried to find a large one that is very ripe. There isn't any reason for this, only that an avocado like that feels as if it should be filled with a strong growing potential. If the fruit you choose isn't really ripe, you can just let it sit for a few days at home until it is. You wouldn't want to eat it until it was soft and ripe anyway. Leave it out in the air, not in the refrigerator. After you have removed the avocado meat without cutting into the pit, you will see a dark slimy film on the pit. Try to wash this off with warm water. Sometimes this covering slides right off. If it doesn't, let the pit sit for a day, so that the skin becomes dry enough to peel off. Do not try to cut the skin off, because you will damage the pit in the process.

Once the film is off, wash the pit well, but be gentle with it. Place three or four wooden toothpicks in the pit about a third of the way down from the pointed end. Place the pit in a widemouth glass or bottle, making sure that the flatter end faces the bottom and that the toothpicks rest on the edge of the container. Fill the glass with warm water so that at least the bottom half of the pit is submerged. You do not want the pointed top to be in water because that is where the main stem will emerge. Now put the container in a dark place. A kitchen cabinet or a closet is the perfect place. Make sure you don't hide it away someplace where you might forget about it. Also be careful to put it where it won't be tipped over when you go to look for it or anything else. Keeping it in the dark forces the seed to grow roots in the water without being distracted by upward growth. The roots should start to appear in about a week; however, I've started pits that have taken two months to root. If you are patient, your avocado will eventually sprout roots as long as you change the water about once a week. Occasionally, a pit may start to rot, in which case you have to throw it away. If the pit develops a slimy, gooey texture and the water gets a scummy green color, you'll know that the pit is beginning to rot. Don't let this possibility discourage you from starting an avocado because it really doesn't happen very often. To avoid disappointment, you can start several pits at the same time and watch how they develop at different rates (see diagram).

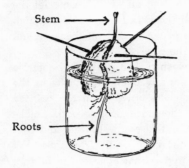

Stem →

Roots →

SPROUTING PIT

When the roots are well on their way, you may see a small sprout beginning to appear between the two sections cracking open at the top of the pit. This is the main stem. Once the stem shows its head, it will grow quite rapidly. It will have a small green bud at the top of a reddish brown stalk. When this stem gets to be seven or eight inches high, you *must* cut it back. This is perhaps the most important part in developing a strong, bushy tree. By cutting back at this early stage, you will be temporarily stunting the upward growth, to ensure additional root growth. Avocados grow to be very large trees, and they need strong roots. Take the tree out of its dark home, and put it on a table. Measure the length of the stem with a ruler. You should cut off about half the stem, leaving three to four inches protruding from the pit. Use a sharp

156

knife to make the diagonal cut. This procedure must be followed even if there are full leaves at the tip of the stem. If you don't cut back now, your avocado is doomed to be of the telephone-pole type. The plant is young enough to recover and to benefit from this ostensibly massive amputation (see diagram).

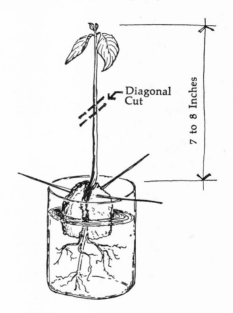

DEVELOPED STEM

Put the seed back in its dark place. The weeks following this operation are crucial to the plant. You will see more roots develop and the old ones thicken. Remember to keep the container filled with water. A new stem will start to grow out just below where you made the cut on the original stem. This is just what

157

you want to happen, although in some cases an entirely new stem will appear out of the pit. Both of these options indicate a healthy future for the avocado.

After you have made the first stem cut, continue to keep the pit in a dark place for two to three weeks. By this time the necessary root growth should have taken place. It is now time to bring the pit into the light. After all the work and care you put into the avocado, you will really feel that you deserve to look at this odd thing. The avocado will grow upward because it will be in soil and will get sunlight. The avocado must now be planted in soil.

How to Plant Avocado in Soil.

1. Prepare a 10- or 12-inch clay pot with shards and charcoal.
2. Fill the pot two-thirds full with potting soil.
3. Carefully remove the toothpicks from the pit. If the picks break off inside, don't try to get them out, because you will bruise the pit. The toothpick will eventually decompose.

PLANTING PIT

4. In one hand, hold the pit by the sides, without hurting the roots or stem, just above the soil (see darker area). The roots should not be crowded down to the soil. With the other hand, carefully put handfuls of soil under and around the roots. Don't pack it down, because the roots might get squashed.

5. Continue to add soil until it covers only two-thirds of the pit (see lighter area). The remaining third will always be exposed to the air so that it will not rot.

6. With the pot in the sink, run tepid water gently onto the soil until it runs out the bottom.

7. Add soil again bringing it to a level two-thirds of the way up the pit.

Your avocado is now in its new home where it can stay until it gets extremely large and you feel it needs to be moved to a larger pot. This probably will not be necessary for several years.

Avocados need a lot of light, preferably sunlight, and a good deal of water. Soak the plant with water as soon as the soil is dry. Spray it often, because it likes a humid climate. The plant may not show signs of growth for a few days after you have potted it: this is normal. It will soon overcome the shocking experience.

When the stem starts to grow and gets to be about 10 inches tall, it will need to be supported if it is to grow straight. Buy a thin 36-inch gardening stake and put it in the soil not too near the pit. If it's too close, it could damage the roots. Tie the stake to the stem with string. Do not pull the string so tight that it could choke the stem.

At the tip of the stem there will be a bud or even some leaves. Pinch this bud as you would any other plant. Continue to pinch every bud you see. This will guarantee a fuller plant by forcing growth below the tip. You may get a new side branch because of all the pinching. Keep a close watch over these too, making

AVOCADO

160

sure to pinch every bud. You can never pinch too many buds on an avocado. It will always create a bushier plant. I still pinch buds off my tree quite frequently. In fact, in the spring I find new buds every day, which I always pinch.

As your avocado grows taller, you may need to get a longer stake because the plant may be falling over the top. If the diameter of the stake is larger than the one you had before, be sure it doesn't smash the roots when you put it in the soil.

If you follow these instructions and remember to pinch the buds whenever they appear, you will have a gorgeous, lush tree within two years that will grow quickly and beautifully. You will feel very proud of yourself for having been patient and courageous in the early months of growing an avocado. The only disappointment about these trees is that they almost never bear avocado fruits in home gardens. You'll just have to buy one if you feel like eating one.

And then you can always start the process over again.

A YAM: INSTEAD OF EATING IT . . .

The yam is a variety of sweet potato. When provided with a continual water supply and allowed to take root, it produces a magnificent vine that multiplies overnight. The growth process is so quick that you can practically see the leaves unfolding. In fact, yams are a delight to watch from their very inception. Children become fascinated watching brightly colored vines grow from a potato they would normally eat. Some people may recall growing yams as young children in kindergarten.

It can be even more enjoyable for you now if your interest in plants is on the rise.

Yam plants have a shorter life span than most houseplants. I have had some that lasted only for about six months. In each case the plant would quickly become extraordinarily thick and profuse, but then its growth rate would slow down and in about two weeks would begin to yellow and die. Other yams I've begun are still flourishing. Some say that yam plants only have a six-month life cycle and will inevitably die after this time elapses. But I have had some growing about a year. The difference seems to be in the growing medium. The plants that thrive are the ones left to grow in water. The yams I've potted in soil are the ones that have been short-lived. Either way, you will have at least a good six months of fabulous foliage unfolding for you.

All the preparation and care is so simple, your best bet is to start three or four yams at once. Some potatoes take more readily than others. All of them will take root and eventually sprout leaves. Even though you start a few simultaneously, they will sprout at different times because each has its own rate of growth. Yams will root more quickly in the months from March to September. During the spring and summer months, roots should form within two to three weeks and sprouting will follow immediately. It will be approximately six weeks before you can count on a full-fledged plant. The yams that I've tried to root after the weather turns colder take months to look like anything worthwhile. The roots, which usually appear first, arrived after the sprouting. The buds were small and took two or three months to open and become vines. Even after the buds formed, the roots were

162

practically nonexistent. So, although yams can be grown at all times of year, the spring and summer months are best.

Go to the supermarket's vegetable section and pick out three or four yams from the potato bins. I have found from experience that the most productive kind are the long, thinly shaped ones rather than the huge round ones. Remember, the biggest ones are not the best. Keep in mind that at first they have to fit into jars or glasses filled with water. If they are large they will be unmanageable. Yams sell for about 29 cents a pound, so this venture will be inexpensive.

When you get them home, wash them carefully and gently with warm water. Make sure to get as much of the surface dirt removed as possible. Don't peel the potato. Take a knife and cut about one-third of the potato off. It does not matter which end is cut. Fill a wide-mouth jar or glass with warm water. It will be best if the container is clear so that light may reach the part of the potato that will be submerged. Place the toothpicks a little more than halfway up from the cut-off base. Force them approximately half their length into the potato. Place them at regular intervals so they will rest easily across the rim of the container. You will need about four picks. Put the potato into the jar with the cut part face down in the water. About one-third of the yam is sticking up from the top of the glass and the rest is underwater. It is absolutely vital to keep the container filled with lukewarm water at all times. Because of evaporation in dry rooms and the amount used by the potato for nourishment, the water level decreases in a matter of a few days. Keep this checked constantly; otherwise, the potato will shrivel up and nothing will grow.

Place the jar on a windowsill or anyplace where it will get a good deal of light. Sun is not necessary, but it can only help. The water may become foggy and mucky. Change it if this happens. The best way to avoid this is to place a small piece of charcoal in the bottom of the glass. It will act as a filter. The bottom of the potato may also become covered with a white fuzzy scum. If this happens to yours, take it out of the water and gently wash it off with your hands. Be careful while doing this: this muck may hide white

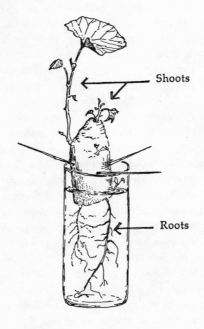

Shoots

Roots

DEVELOPING YAM

roots. The roots are fragile at first and may be mistaken for fuzz, so examine the cut-off part well before you take any drastic steps. It will take a few weeks before you will see a network of stringy, white roots growing out the sides and bottom of the yam. At this time you will also see deep purple and green sprouts appearing all over the potato. Some will grow on top, while others will spring out from the submerged surface.

As these purplish red shoots grow, you will notice they are really leaves folded in half. The leaf will gradually unfold and grow larger and lighter in color, until the purple disappears and a bright apple green takes its place. Each sprout reproduces itself until the growth takes on the appearance of a vine. The stem becomes woodier or more barklike as it matures. The stem closest to the yam becomes stiff and brown, while the new growth is soft and green. This process occurs all over the potato, so you can imagine how lovely and profuse it will look after a while. You can train the vines to grow upward with a stick, or you can use a piece of string to hold the plant gently against the wall. Otherwise, for those who like hanging vines, just let them drop over the edge of the container.

It is optional at this point to pot the yam in soil or leave it in water. As the plant grows the vines become very cumbersome and even top-heavy, so your original jar may not hold it. Change the yam to a larger container, giving the roots and the vines plenty of room to grow. If you want, pot the yam in soil in a seven- or eight-inch pot. Place the potato in the pot with one hand and push the soil all around it with the other. It is necessary to hold the potato up so that the elaborate root system doesn't get crushed. Don't be afraid though: the roots are strong and hardy. Make sure

MATURE YAM

the top of the potato sticks up above the soil. Use the same principle as you did in the container and water instructions. Soak the potted plant with water and let it drain. Always keep a large dish of water underneath the pot, as a constant water supply. The yam is a fast-growing plant and demands an enormous amount of water; without enough water, the leaves will droop immediately. This is why it is best to leave the potato in water. This will make things easier for you and provide more beneficial conditions for the plant.

These yams make wonderful gifts at any stage in their life cycle. It is especially fun to give a newly sprouting and rooting yam to a friend. This way you give someone the pleasure of watching an enormous plant develop from a little cut-off potato.

A TERRARIUM: HOW TO . . .

Throughout the book, terrariums have been mentioned as a viable alternative to greenhouse conditions for plants such as ferns, marantas, fittonias, and African violets. A terrarium can be any size but must be transparent like glass or clear plastic. You can use a fish tank, decorative bottles, an old-fashioned jar, or even fancy drinking glasses. Just make sure you have something to use as a lid that will fit securely over the top of the container. You can use a bottle with a very narrow neck but it will be very difficult to plant even with tweezers. Ideally, you will be most comfortable at first with a container you can fit your hand into without too much trouble. Especially in your initial attempts at arranging a terrarium, don't make the operation demand more patience than it already does.

The idea behind the terrarium is that by enclosing a container on all sides and keeping it covered, a warm, humid environment similar to a greenhouse is created for plants that simply won't survive in the dry conditions of centrally heated homes. You are creating a miniature jungle that needs hardly any care after the task of putting it together. You can watch everything grow from the outside, while the terrarium manufactures its own food, moist air, and water. It will hardly ever need feeding, if at all. It can generally go for months without watering. Propagation takes care of itself.

Here's how to make one. It's really simple, although time-consuming, so try not to be scared off by what may seem to be more complex than it really is. Begin by finding yourself a transparent container that pleases you. Line the bottom of it with two or three inches of pebbles or gravel to create drainage, as you would in the bottom of a pot. Some people say this level is not necessary, that simply sterilized potting soil will suffice. From my own experience, I do not think this the case. Many of the cuttings I planted rotted from lack of drainage. So, if you want your terrarium to last for more than a week and the foliage to flourish, use a layer of pebbles or gravel at the bottom. Something that isn't necessary but certainly will enhance your terrarium is charcoal. If you mix a few handfuls of charcoal in with the gravel, it will keep the water from smelling rotten and generally act as a filter. I have also had advice from those who know the intricacies of terrariums that over this layer you should spread some sand (about two inches) before adding rich potting soil. This is up to you. Mix some sphagnum or peat moss together with general potting soil for the top layer. The amount depends on how you want to arrange your little forest or jungle scene. You can make it all one level or build some parts higher than others. Since the terrarium environment encourages all growth, it is a good idea to sterilize the soil if it isn't prepackaged. Otherwise, bacteria will multiply rapidly. Sterilize by baking the soil in the oven on a tray or pan for half an hour at 200 degrees.

Moisten the soil slowly and carefully so that you don't overwater it. You'll know it s ready if, when you stick a pencil in deep to make a hole, the hole doesn't fill up with water. The earth should be moist but not waterlogged.

Besides the plants already mentioned that take well to a terrarium, almost anything can be put inside. You can plant seeds from fruits like oranges and grapefruits or cuttings from plants around the house. Plant a small pot of baby tears, which are always in need of moisture. Fittonia, moss from the woods, or almost anything you can dig up from a natural area are usable. Unless you are using a huge container, put only small plants inside. The terrarium atmosphere stimulates growth to such a degree that too large a plant will outgrow the container in no time.

After you have your landscape arranged to your liking, give the whole thing a fine misting. Cover the container with its lid or place a plate, sheet of glass, or plastic wrap over the opening. After a few hours the glass may get misty, but that is normal. If there's a great deal of water near the top or if it is so cloudy you can't see, then take off the cover and let it dry out for a while. Only you will know when it is time to put the cover back on. It should only take a few hours. Most likely your new terrarium will not need watering for about one month. Don't put it in the sun or a well-heated place. It will make the temperature inside the container too great, killing the plants. Indirect light or artificial light is sufficient. One last word of caution: when you choose your container make sure the glass or plastic is not distorting. The first terrarium I made was a great source of pride to me until I set it in its place to admire it. Then I realized the glass was too thick (it was an old cookie jar) and I couldn't see my creation clearly. It was like looking into a fun-house mirror.

A NEW PLANT: WHAT TO LOOK FOR

Once you have begun a garden at home, you will be tempted to buy more plants each time you pass a florist. Most plants look gorgeous in the shop because there are thousands of lovely, lush greens all bunched together. Unfortunately for the buyer, they never look as good when you get them home. So you have to beware of several things when buying your next plant.

Usually you will be attracted to the plants that have very shiny leaves because they seem healthier. Don't be fooled by this: it is common practice for the florist to treat the leaves with a chemical that makes the plant appear healthy even though it may not be.

Never buy a plant with drooping, discolored leaves. It means the florist doesn't know how to care, or hasn't cared, for the plant. One good way to insure getting a strong plant is to buy from a shop that keeps it's plants in the sun. Often the plants are kept in the back of the shop and never get enough light and air. Talk to the florist. Find out how involved he or she is with the plants. If he or she is more involved with selling flowers and fancy arrangements, there is a good chance he knows nothing more about plants than how much profit they yield.

On the other hand, there are many shopkeepers who are committed to their plants and the success of them in your home. These people will talk to you about plants you already have. They will answer your questions, and won't push you to buy the most expensive plant in the store.

Pick out plants that are bushy and full. In the case of flowering plants, like begonias or geraniums, choose plants that have only buds and not full flowers. Your chances of seeing the flowers for a longer time at home will be greatly increased with many small buds.

When you bring the plant home try not to shock it any more than is absolutely necessary. The plant needs to get adjusted to its new home. If you want to transfer the plant into a new pot, *don't* do it immediately. Wait at least a week so that the plant doesn't feel it has too many new conditions to contend with. Also, it is best not to water the plant right away. There are good reasons for this: first, you don't know what its needs are, and second, the plant will not act its normal self until it is completely adjusted to your home conditions.

Before you buy the plant, check to see that it is not infested by pests. If you see hairy white spots, green larvae, spider webs, or unusual brown spots, don't buy the plant. In fact, if you see such creatures, don't buy anything in that shop. There is a good chance that many plants in that store have pests. In such crowded conditions, it is very easy for bugs to infect neighboring plants. Then the infestation can only snowball. Find another plant store.

Many people like to isolate new plants for a time when they bring them home. This way they can watch for any unhealthy signs without risking contamination of the other plants. When they are sure the plant is healthy, they let it join the others. I prefer to introduce a new plant to my present collection as soon as I bring it home. I want to make it feel comfortable right away. Plants grow better when they are together. I can still keep a close watch on the new member of my plant family to see that it is pest-free and grows healthy and strong.

9 WHAT TO DO WHEN YOU GO AWAY

WEEKENDS AND VACATIONS

Most people think that the best thing to do when going on vacation is to ask a friend to take care of the plants. Actually, this is not a sure thing when you consider that your friend is not familiar with the watering cycle of your plants. You know how long it took you to get to know your plants. It is a difficult situation for a friend to take over the care and maintenance of your collection. The chances are good that overwatering will be the result unless your friend really knows what he's doing. But if you prefer to do it this way, you can be helpful to your plants and your friend by making out a small index card describing each plant and the kind of treatment it expects. For instance, a friend of mine overwatered my hanging spider plant while I was away. It turned limp and yellow. It took a few weeks for it to dry out and regain its turgidity. The next time I went away I taped an index card on its pot saying, "I am a spider plant. Leave me in the light. I like to be soaked with water and then left to dry out before I am watered again. Too much water makes me limp." This may sound corny, but it worked. I did it with every plant. I believe that the extra care I took meant something to the plants and provided my friend with invaluable assistance. Another card read, "I am a *Coleus*. I like a great deal of water because I am a fast growing plant. Water me whenever you can. I go limp when I need water." I got to know my plants better and got a kick out of compiling all the information that way.

There is another, and possibly more reliable, method for plant care and maintenance while you are away: making a bathtub terrarium. Place some plastic cleaning bags at the bottom of the bathtub. Cover this with about five layers of newspaper. Soak the newspapers thoroughly with water as you lay them down or from the top layer after you have finished putting them all down.

Soak all your plants with water and then place them on top of the newspapers. Then give them all a light shower. This will wet the leaves and add a little extra water to the entire setup. It is all right to crowd the plants. They actually like being close together in a hot, moist environment. Then cover the top of the tub with a couple of layers of clear plastic and seal it up all around the edges to avoid any air seeping in. Make sure there are no holes in the plastic. There is plenty of air and moisture sealed up inside. A greenhouse effect occurs within a few minutes. A mistiness develops underneath the balloonlike plastic window.

You have made yourself a perfect environment for your plants. Leave the light on in the bathroom or hook up a fluorescent or reflector bulb with a clamp fixture. Any kind of light will do. This arrangement will last approximately two weeks. Most of the plants will not grow but rather will be maintained. Others may flourish because of the moisture. In any case, they can't help but do well because you have provided them with everything they need and have not depended on someone else.

One way to care for those plants that do not fit in the tub is to place a plastic bag over the plant and seal it tightly to the pot. If you have watered and sprayed the plant beforehand, you will be creating the same greenhouse atmosphere that you created in the bathtub terrarium. When you get home, open the bag but leave the plant partially covered for a few days. If you took the bag off immediately it would be a tremendous shock to the plant. When the acclimatizing period is over, water the plant well—it will need it.

If a bathtub terrarium is too much trouble for you to make, here's another way of dealing with going away: Place *all* your plants on the floor away from radiators and light. The less light, the better, although complete darkness isn't necessary. Without light, the plants cannot carry on photosynthesis to make them grow. In a way, you are imposing a dormant period on them. They will not grow, but neither will they die. Soak all the plants thoroughly. Saturate the soil because this is all the water your plants will be receiving until you come home. By placing them on the floor, they will be getting the coolest air available. Hot air dries out the foliage and the soil very quickly. If the plants stay on the floor, they will remain moist much longer. Because photosynthesis has been interrupted and the air is cool, the plants can tolerate less water. Mist everything well before you leave and keep a window open slightly to provide the fresh air necessary for breathing.

It isn't imperative that you cover any of the plants

with a plastic bag, but if there are any fragile ferns or fittonia, it is probably a good idea. A friend of mine left her plants like this for two weeks, without bags, and she didn't lose a plant. Not only that, but some of the plants still had moisture in the soil when she got home. Remember, some leaves will drop, yellow, brown, or wilt. Don't worry, it is to be expected. After all, if you aren't around to give them care and attention, there has to be a major change in their living situation. Just clean them up and make them shine. You are home, and that is what really matters.

AFTER-THE-WEEKEND BLUES

Certainly, everyone is familiar with the sinking feeling you get when you come home after a long weekend and all your plants have drooped down to the floor, turned yellow, or have crunchy, brown leaves hanging from limp stems and branches. Most people assume the plants are dead or will be soon. Either the plants are thrown out or not given the proper care, because you gave up on them. Once you have given up on a plant there is usually no hope for it. If you assume it's a lost cause, then it will be: it becomes a self-fulfilling prophecy. I have done this a number of times. If a plant isn't growing but rather sits dormant for months and months, I get very angry at it and frustrated. I used to separate it from the rest of the plants and promptly forget to water it on a regular basis. Every so often, when I felt guilty, I would splash some water on it. Naturally, its condition never improved, but it did make things worse, thereby satisfying all my suspicions of its inadequacy. I'd just get angrier at it and pay less and less attention to it. Finally, it would die, and I would feel relief because I never liked the plant anyway. At last, I could throw it out.

When you do come home after a few days away during which your plants were not provided for, they will need some immediate care. Most of the plants will simply be suffering from lack of water. Soak them all thoroughly, following the directions in the section on watering. Give them all a good spray to revitalize them. You may have left the windows closed or only partially open, depriving the plants of their usual amount of air. If it isn't the dead of winter, open the windows and let your plants breathe! Next, check out all your plants for yellow or brown leaves. Pick them all off, but don't be overzealous. Since many of the plants will be limp from lack of water, wait before removing any leaves that are drooping but haven't changed color. Within a couple of hours, all the plants should return to normal. If you have gone away for more than a few days, some plants go into shock. This can happen as readily when a plant has been under-watered as when it has been overwatered. Your plant is in shock if the leaves remain limp and lifeless even hours after it has been watered. The best thing to do is to leave the plant alone. Take it out of the sun or light and place it in the shade. Treat it as if it were a healthy plant, watering it as you usually would. It is just trying to get itself together after a traumatic experience. This process will take time. The plant should return to normal in less than a week. Some-times, it will take longer, so don't be overly anxious.

You will be amazed at how quickly plants that look hopeless will revive with a little help. My zebra plant, which needs a great deal of water, was practically hanging down to the floor, upside down, after one weekend this summer. The leaves were lifeless, and the stem, which is usually firm and hard, was behaving as if made of rubber. I thought I had lost it. I soaked it with water, and much to my surprise it slowly brought itself up to a standing position. It happened so quickly—within a couple of hours—that I saw it in the various stages of its rise to its full height. It reminded me of time-lapse photographs of a flower blooming over a long period of time. This phenomenon will happen with all plants limp from lack of water. Before you know it, they pull themselves up to their natural stature.

NINE
OVERSIMPLIFICATIONS

Dormancy. All plants have dormant periods. This is the time their growth slows down or stops. When this happens, decrease the water supply. They will not use much in this sleeping or resting state. Buds can be dormant too.

Fronds. The leaves of ferns and palms are called fronds. Each frond is made up of many separate small leaves as in maidenhair, boston ferns, and all palms.

Node. The node is the point on the stem at which the leaf emerges. It resembles the knot or swelling in the trunk of a tree. It is a joint in the stem like a joint in your arm. It is here that the fastest growth takes place. When cutting back a stem, always cut just above a node. New branches begin their growth at nodes.

Offsets. Offsets are miniature replicas of the mother plant. Spider plants, sansevierias, and sempervivums will form offsets if given enough space to propagate.

Phototropism. The ability or tendency of a plant to turn toward its light source is phototropism. Some plants do this at a faster rate than others. Coleus, for example, turns toward the light completely by the end of the day. Other plants take days or weeks to display a noticeable tilt. For this reason, plants must be regularly rotated to preserve the natural shape of the plant.

Photosynthesis. The process by which plants convert light into food energy is photosynthesis. This occurs when light falls on the foliage. In poor light, leaf and root activity will be slow because the plant is not receiving the energy stimulus.

Root hairs. These are the tiny feeding roots along the ends of every main root. Only root hairs absorb the nutrients and moisture necessary to a plant's growth.

Shock. Shock is a temporary disruption of a plant's life processes, causing the leaves to become limp and lacking in turgidity. Your plant can be traumatized by overwatering, underwatering, a draft, repotting, or adjusting to a new home. Sometimes a stem cutting will go into shock when placed in a glass if the water is too cold or simply from the trauma of being cut. This shock will pass, so don't throw out your plant. Sometimes it takes over a week for the plant to return to normal.

Turgidity. The natural swollen state of a plant. When your plant has just been watered, it stands erect and is bouncy to the touch—it's turgid. It is strong and swollen with water, making it seem inflated. All healthy plants are turgid. When they are turgid they are happy.

FOURTEEN PRETTY POISONOUS PLANTS

(Please note that many of the plants included in this chart are not discussed in the book. However, for those of you who have young children or pets who might try to eat your plants, this general information may be useful.)

PLANT	TOXIC PART	SYMPTOMS
Dieffenbachia Crown of thorns Philodendron	All parts	Intense burning and irritation of the mouth and tongue that can cause suffocation
Rhododendron Azalea Laurel	All parts	Nausea, vomiting, depression, difficult breathing; can be fatal
Daphne	Berries	Fatal
Wisteria	Seeds, pods	Mild to severe digestive upset
Hyacinth Narcissus Daffodil	Bulbs	Nausea, vomiting, diarrhea
Oleander	Leaves, branches	Affects heart, severe digestive upset; extremely poisonous
Jasmine	Berries	Digestive and nervous symptoms; can be fatal.
Yew	Berries, foliage	Foliage more toxic than berries; can be fatal

CHART COURTESY OF SUSAN GRAD

INDEX

Pages with illustrations are listed in *italics*.

Adiantum, *see* Ferns

African Violet, 16, 18, 87, 111, *111*, 112, 113, 146, 167

Air-layering, 55, 125, 148–151

Aloe, 31–32

Aluminum Plant, 55–57, *56*, 65, 68

Aphelandra, *see* Zebra Plant

Aphids, 94, 95

Aralia, *see* False Aralia

Araucaria, *see* Norfolk Island Pine

Artificial light, 8–11, 112

Asparagus Fern, 14, 16, 97–99, *97*, 146

Aspidistra, *see* Cast Iron Plant

Avocado, 18, 71, 154–161, *160*

Azalea, 179

Baby Tears, 169

Begonia, 16, 18, 65, 70, 130–134, *131*, 146

Boston Fern, *see* Ferns

Butterfly Palm, 64

Buying plants, 170–171

Cacti, 7, 32–35, *33*

Caladium, 138–139, *138*

Carbon dioxide, 86

Cast Iron Plant, 26–27, *26*

Central heating, 14

Ceropegia, *see* Rosary Vine

Charcoal, 75, 133, 168

Chlorophytum, *see* Spider Plant

Cissus, *see* Grape Ivy

Cleaning plants, 16–18

Cockroaches, 96

Codiaeum, *see* Croton

Coleus, 11, 18, 56, 65, 68, 82, 118–119, *118*, 146, 173

Columnea, 35–36, *35*

Compost, 84

Crassula, *see* Jade Plant

Croton, 7, 128–130, *129*

Crown of Thorns, 179

Cutting back, 67–72

Daffodil, 179

Daphne, 179

Diazianon, 93–97

Dieffenbachia, *see* Dumb Cane

Division, 39, 99, 146–148

Dizygotheca, *see* False Aralia

Dormancy, 66, 68, 174, 177

Dracaena, 4, 5, 20–23, *23*, 71, 148

Dumb Cane, 18, 53–55, *54*, 71, 148, 179

Echeveria, 31

English Ivy, 7, *109*, 110, 153

Euphorbia, 33

Exposures, windows, 6–8

False Aralia, 27–28, *28*

Feeding, 85–90

Ferns, 18, 94, 99–103, *100*, *101*, 146, 167

Fertilizer, *see* Feeding

Ficus, *see* Rubber Plant

Fig tree, *see* Rubber Plant

Fittonia, 16, 134–135, *134*, 146, 167, 169

Footcandle, 3, 6

Frond, 102, 103, 177

Geranium, 7, 16, 18, 65, 71, 120–122, *120*

Grapefruit, 169

Grape Ivy, 109, *109*

Greenhouse, 173, 174

Gynura, *see* Velvet Plant

Hedera, *see* English Ivy, 110

Humus, 83

Humidity, 14

Hyacinth, 179

Ivy, 18, 108–111, *109*

Jade Plant, 7, 65, 94, 104–107, *105*

Jasmine, 179

Kalanchoe, 32, *94*

Laurel, 179

Light, 3–11

Maidenhair Fern, *see* Ferns

Malathion, 93–97

Manure, 86

Maranta, *see* Prayer Plant
Marble Queen, 51–53, *52*, 151
Mealy bugs, 93, *94*, 130
Mite, cyclamen, 95
Mite, red spider, *94*, 130
Monstera, 18, 57–59, *57*, 151

Narcissus, 179
Nephrolepsis, *see* Boston Fern
Nepthytis, 4, 18, 59–60, *59*, 151
Nicotine solution, 96
Nicotine sulphate, 95
Nitrogen, 86
Node, 69, 177
Norfolk Island Pine, 139–141, *140*

Offsets, 146, 178
Oleander, 179
Opuntia, 35
Orange seed, 169
Overfeeding, 89
Overwatering, 12–15

Palm, 18, 60–64, 71
    Butterfly, 63, 64
    Chinese Fan, 62, *63*, 64
    Parlor, 63, 64
    Sentry, *61*, 64
Parlor Ivy, *109*, 110–111
Peat moss, 85
Pelargonium, *see* Geranium
Peperomia, 47–49, *47*
Perlite, 84
Pests, 90–96
Philodendron, 4, 18, 23–26, *24*, 146, 151, 179
Phosphoric acid, 86
Photosynthesis, 10, 174, 178
Phototropism, 11, 119, 137, 178
Piggyback Plant, 18, 115–117, *116*
Pilea, *see* Aluminum Plant
Pinching, 65–67, *66*, 119, 122
Platycerium, *see* Staghorn Fern
Plectranthus, *see* Swedish Ivy
Plumosus, *see* Asparagus Fern
Poisonous plants, 179
Potash, 86
Pot-bound, 72–73, *73*
Pothos, *see* Marble Queen
Pots, 79–82
Prayer Plant, 36–39, *37*, 88, 146
Pruning, *see* Cutting back; Pinching
Propagation, 142–153
Purple Passion Plant, *see* Velvet plant

Repotting, 72–79

Rhododendron, 179
Root ball, 76–77, *77*
Root hairs, 72, 178
Rooting, 69
Root-pruning, 71
Roots, 83
Rosary Vine, 107–108, *107*, 151, 153
Rubber plant, 18, 122–125, *123*, 148
Runners, 147

Saintpaulia, *see* African Violet
Sand, 85, *see also* Perlite
Sansevieria, 4, 44–46, *45*, 146
Scales, 94
Scindapsus, *see* Marble Queen
Schefflera, *see* Umbrella Tree
Sedum, 30–31
Semperflorens, 132, 133
Sempervivum, 32
Senecio, *see* Parlor Ivy
Shards, 75
Shock, 78–79, *79*, 176, 178
Snake plant, *see* Sansevieria
Soil, 83–85
Spathiphyllum, 42–45, *43*, 146
Sphagnum moss, 85
Spider Plant, 49–51, *49*, 146
Spores, 94, 102–103
Spraying, 15–17
Sprengeri, *see* Asparagus Fern
Staghorn Fern, 103–104, *103*
Stem cuttings, 128, 134, 137, 142–146
Sterilized soil, 168
Succulents, 7, 28–32, *30*, 108
Swedish Ivy, 18, 67, 68, 125–128, *125*, 146, 151
Sweet Potato, *see* Yam
Syngonium, *see* Nepthytis

Talking to plants, 2
Terrarium, 38, 100, 115, 135
    bathtub, 173
    how-to, 167–169
Tolmiea, *see* Piggyback Plant
Top-heavy, 73–74, *74*
Tradescantia, *see* Wandering Jew
Transplanting, *see* Repotting
Turgidity, 78, 172, 178

Umbrella Tree, 39–40, *39*

Vacations, 172–177
Velvet plant, 41–42, *41*
Vermiculite, 144, 145

Wandering Jew, 18, 68, 135–138, *136*, 146, 151
Watering, 12–15
Weekends, *see* Vacations
White flies, 95
Winding and pinning, 108, 151–153
Wisteria, 179

Yam, 161–167, *164*, *166*
Yew, 179

Zebra plant, 56, 65, 68, 113–115, *113*, 176
Zebrina, *see* Wandering Jew